Mediaeval Philosophical Texts in Translation

No. 33

Roland J. Teske, S.J., Editor
Lee C. Rice, Assistant Editor

Editorial Board

Lee C. Rice
Mary F. Rousseau
John L. Treloar, S.J.
Wanda Zemler-Cizewski

Francisco Suárez

# ON BEINGS OF REASON

# (De Entibus Rationis)

# Metaphysical Disputation LIV

Translated from the Latin

with an Introduction and Notes

by

John P. Doyle

Marquette University Press
Milwaukee, Wisconsin

© 1995, Marquette University Press
Printed in the United States of America
ISBN 0-87462-236-0
Library of Congress Catalogue Card Number: 94-72904

Second printing, 2004

TO MARY GALE

WITH LOVE AND GRATITUDE

## Table of Contents

Acknowledgements .................................................................... ix
I.   Suárez -- The Man, his Work, and his Influence ............... 1
II.  Introduction to the 54th Disputation ................................... 17
III. Translation Notes ................................................................ 55
IV.  Disputation 54 – On Beings of Reason ............................. 57
     Prologue. Why We Are Treating Here Of Beings Of Reason ......... 57
     Section I: Whether being of reason exists, and what
          essence it could have ...................................... 59
     Section II: Whether a Being of Reason has a Cause,
          and of what kind that may be ......................... 66
     Section III: Whether Being of Reason is Rightly
          Divided into Negation, Privation, and Relation ......... 84
     Section IV: Whether Being of Reason is Sufficiently
          Divided into Negation, Privation, and Relation ......... 90
     Section V: How Negations and Privations Agree or
          Differ inasmuch as they are Beings of Reason ......... 98
     Section VI: What is Necessary for a Relation of
          Reason, and in How Many Ways may it be
          Fashioned or Contrived? ................................ 116

Bibliography ............................................................................ 123

Index of Names ....................................................................... 131

Index of Terms ........................................................................ 135

# Acknowledgements

I want to express my gratitude to the following persons: first, to Professor Jorge J. E. Gracia of the State University of New York at Buffalo, whose suggestion it was to begin this work; then to my old friend and teacher, Professor Norman J. Wells of Boston College, who almost four decades ago introduced me to Francisco Suárez; and to Professor Donald Cress of the University of Illinois at DeKalb, who generously provided me with a copy of Disputation 54 from the Salamanca, 1597, edition. A special word of thanks is due to Father Theodore Vitali, C.P., Chairman of the Department of Philosophy at St. Louis University, who lightened my teaching load to give me time to complete this project. Again I have special thanks for Father Roland Teske, S.J., Editor of Marquette University's Mediaeval Philosophical Texts in Translation, for his patient and painstaking editorial work on this volume. Finally, I thank my wife, Mary Gale, and our children, who have always loved me and encouraged my work.

# I. Suárez – The Man, his Work, and his Influence

Francisco Suárez was born at Granada in Spain on January 5, 1548.[1] With the reception of tonsure, at the early age of ten he started toward an ecclesiastical career.[2] Following three years of preparatory studies, in the autumn of 1561 he enrolled at what was then the finest university in the world, viz., Salamanca.[3] Here he studied law until at sixteen years of age he heard the call of God and entered, on the 16th of June, 1564, into the recently founded Society of Jesus.[4] However, of fifty students from Salamanca who applied for admission to the Jesuits in 1564, Suárez alone was rejected as not bright enough. The fact is almost impossible to explain but nonetheless true.[5] The only plausible explanation seems to be that, entering on his legal studies at too early an age, he was not outstanding at them and this caused his examiners to doubt his ability.[6] Not daunted, however, by their verdict, young Francisco appealed to the Jesuit Provincial Superior of Castille, Juan Suárez (no relation), who heard him with sympathy.[7] Following this he was accepted into the Society on June 16, 1584, but as an "indifferent," a title reserved for those admitted without any decision made as to whether they would be ordained priests or kept on only as lay brothers.[8] Indeed, it has been cited as "a matter of later history" that Suárez asked to remain a lay brother in the Society of Jesus "since he himself was convinced that he could not successfully complete even the fundamental courses in philosophy."[9]

---

1. See R. De Scorraille, S.J., *François Suarez de la Compagnie de Jésus* (Paris, 1911), I, 3. This work is still the chief source for Suárez's life. In English see Joseph Fichter, *Man of Spain, Francis Suarez* (New York, 1940), 6. For a briefer but still accurate presentation, cf. P. Monnot, "Suarez, François. I. Vie et oeuvres," *Dictionnaire de Théologie Catholique*, XIV, 2e partie (Paris, 1941) cols. 2638-2649. On Suárez's ancestry cf., José de Duenas, S.J., "Los Suárez de Toledo," *Razón y Fe*, número extraordinario (Madrid, 1948), pp. 91-110. For recent presentations of Suárez in his historical setting, cf. Jorge J. E. Gracia, "Francisco Suárez: The Man in History," *The American Catholic Philosophical Quarterly*, LXV (1991), pp. 259-266; and Carlos Noreña, "Suárez and the Jesuits," *ibid.*, pp. 267-286.
2. De Scorraille, I, 3.
3. De Scorraille, I, 30; Fichter, 29.
4. De Scorraille, I, 45-46; Fichter, 48-50.
5. De Scorraille, I, 43; Fichter, 38.
6. De Scorraille, I, 44.
7. De Scorraille, I, 45-46; Fichter, 48-50.
8. De Scorraille, I, 48; Fichter, 51.
9. Fichter, 52.

In any event, about two weeks after his reception into the Jesuits, Suárez made his way to the noviatiate at Medina del Campo,[10] where, after only three months,[11] his true caliber was to some extent recognized and he was sent by his Jesuit superiors back to the Society's College at Salamanca to begin at seventeen the study of philosophy.[12] At first Suárez was not a noteworthy philosopher.[13] But in a short time his brilliance became apparent, so much so that the following year (1565) when the later famous Gregory of Valencia (1550-1603) entered the Society Suárez was made his tutor.[14]

In August, 1566, Suárez took his first vows as a Jesuit and then went on to theological studies, still at Salamanca, in October of the same year.[15] Since at that time the Jesuits did not yet have enough theologians to staff the faculties under which their students were enrolled, it happened that Suárez's class received a rather eclectic but, nevertheless, first-rate training from different professors on the University faculty of theology.[16] Chief among his mentors here was the Dominican, Juan Mancio (1497-1576), who was himself first a pupil and then, in Salamanca's principal chair (*cathedra de prima*) of theology, a successor of the great Francisco de Vitoria, O.P (1492/3-1546).[17]

Following his theological studies, Suárez in 1570 began to teach philosophy, initially at Salamanca as a scholastic tutor,[18] and then as a regular

---

10. De Scorraille, I, 49.
11. "... an uncommonly short time ...." Fichter, 53.
12. De Scorraille, I, 52; Fichter, 53.
13. Fichter, 62.
14. *Ibid.*, 70.
15. De Scorraille, I, 84.
16. Fichter, 79.
17. "Perhaps in no other university in the world is there to be found so brilliant a succession of professors as that which filled the principal chair of theology at Salamanca during the sixteenth century. Suarez' teacher, Mancio, was the fifth of the line which started with the great Francis Vittorio in 1526, and ended with the controversial Dominic Banez in 1604. In the order in which they followed Vittorio these outstanding Dominican scholars were: Melchior Cano, Dominic de Soto, Peter de Sotomayor, John Mancio, Bartholomew de Medina, and Dominic Banez. All of these men enter intimately into the life of Francis Suarez; those before Mancio, his teacher, because of their influence on his development; those after Mancio because he knew them personally and was sometimes at odds with them." Fichter, 79-80. On Vitoria, cf. F. Alluntis, (O.F.M.) "Vitoria, Francisco de," *The Encyclopedia of Philosophy*, VIII, pp. 256-257; C. McKenna, "Vitoria, Francisco de," *New Catholic Encyclopedia* (New York, 1967), XIV, pp. 727-728. Further information about these sixteenth century occupants of the *cathedra de prima* in the University of Salamanca may be gleaned from John O. Riedl, *et al.*, *A Catalogue of Renaissance Philosophers (1350-1650)* (Milwaukee: Marquette University Press, 1940), 72-74.
18. De Scorraille, I, 118.

professor in the Jesuit College at Segovia.[19] – It was here that he was ordained a priest in March of 1572.[20] After ordination, he continued to lecture in philosophy until, in September, 1574, at the Jesuit College, Valladolid, he commenced his main life's work as a theology teacher.[21] Later he taught theology at Avila (1575), Segovia (1575), Valladolid again (1576), Rome (1580), Alcalá (1585), and Salamanca (1593).[22]

Meanwhile, in 1581, Philip II of Spain had combined the kingdoms of Spain and Portugal.[23] It was sixteen years after this that Suárez, complying with a request by Philip to the Jesuits, assumed in 1597 the principal chair of theology at the University of Coimbra.[24] Here he remained, teaching and participating in theological discussions, until his retirement at the end of the academic year, 1614-1615.[25] At this time he became a "jubilarian professor," the equivalent of a modern "professor emeritus."[26] Two years later – on the 25th of September, 1617 – he died in Lisbon.[27]

While he lived, Suárez took part in a number of theological and political controversies. Perhaps the most famous of these was the controversy *De auxiliis* ("On the Helps [for Salvation]"), which occurred in the sixteenth century between the Jesuits and the Dominicans concerning God's foreknowledge and causality, grace, and human freedom. In this Suárez was loyal to his own Order and was one of its principal representatives, along with Robert Bellarmine (1542-1621) and Luis Molina (1535-1600).[28]

Less doctrinal and in some respects more political was the dispute between the Republic of Venice and the papacy about the limits of papal jurisdiction. In defense of the papal position, Suárez in 1607 composed (but did not publish) a treatise, more than one hundred and fifty pages in folio, entitled, *De immunitate ecclesiastica a Venetis violata* ("About the ecclesiastical immunity violated by the Venetians").[29] For this effort he

---

19. De Scorraille, I, 130ff; Fichter, 94.
20. De Scorraille, I, 133; Fichter, 96.
21. De Scorraille, I, 149; Fichter, 107.
22. Cf. Fichter, 107-198.
23. On this, see e.g. John Lynch, *Spain under the Habsburgs: Volume One: Empire and Absolutism 1516-1598*, 2nd edition (New York, 1984), pp. 322-330.
24. De Scorraille, I, 335ff.; Fichter, 208.
25. De Scorraille, II, 223; Fichter, 325-327.
26. Cf. *ibid*.
27. *Ibid*.
28. For a succinct account of this controversy, in which, however, Suárez is unfortunately omitted, see Antonio Astrain, "Congregatio de Auxiliis," *Catholic Encyclopedia*, IV (New York, 1913), 238-239. On the role of Suárez, De Scorraille says (I, 350): "... acteur de seconde ordre seulement si on en juge par les apparences, il l'est en réalité de première ordre, si on tient compte de l'influence qu'il exerça par ses écrits et par ses conseils."
29. De Scorraille, II, 122. Fichter, 271. This treatise was later published in part by Msgr. Malou in a compilation entitled: *Francisci Suarezii opuscula sex inedita* (Bruxelles et Paris, 1859).

received a letter of commendation from Pope Paul V in which it was stated that the work revealed its author as "an eminent and pious theologian." From this has come the honorific title with which Suárez has passed into history – *Doctor eximius ac pius* ("Outstanding and pious Teacher").[30]

As for Suárez's other works[31] – the first of these was published at Alcalá in 1590 by Pedro Madrigal and was entitled: *Commentariorum ac disputationum in tertiam partem divi Thomae. Tomus primus* ("The First Tome of Commentaries and Disputations[32] on the Third Part of St. Thomas").[33] It was a commentary on the first twenty-six questions of the third part (IIIa) of the *Summa Theologiae* of St. Thomas,[34] called by Suárez, *De Verbo Incarnato* ("On the Incarnate Word").[35] After two years, he followed this volume with a continuation of the same commentary, this time titled, *De mysteriis vitae Christi* ("On the Mysteries of Christ's Life").[36] Thus was inaugurated an intense labor which resulted in volume after volume appearing in Suárez's own lifetime or left to be published posthumously by his friend and literary executor, Baltasar Alvarez (1561-1630).[37] The extent of this labor can be seen from any of the several

---

30. De Scorraille, II, 126-127; Fichter, 272.
31. What follows is not meant to be a complete list of Suárez's writings, which would include such items as letters and manuscripts of different types which are as yet unedited. For relatively complete lists of the works of Suárez with dates of their publication, see M. Solana, *Historia de la filosofía española, epoca del Renacimiento* (Madrid, 1941), III, 455 ff.; and J. Iturrioz, "Bibliografía suareciana," *Pensamiento*, número extraordinario (Madrid, 1948), 603ff.
32. The Latin word, *disputatio*, presents a minor problem for an English translator. Here and in what follows I have rendered it with the English word, "disputation." There is, however, nothing acrimonious about Suárez's *Disputationes* – a character which might be suggested by "disputation" in English. Perhaps the most fitting English word would be "discussion," which I have not used only for the reason that I wanted to stay as close in form to Suárez's word as possible. On the role of the disputation in early Jesuit education, with citations from the *Ratio studiorum* of 1586 and the *Ratio studiorum* of 1599, together with 17th century criticism of Scholastic disputations, cf. E. Gilson, *René Descartes: Discours de la Méthode, texte et commentaire* (Paris, 1947), pp. 135-6.
33. De Scorraille, I, 251, n. 4.
34. In his early works Suárez reproduced the text of the *Summa*, followed it with a commentary, and then added a series of "Disputations." The commentary normally is brief while the Disputations are usually of considerable length. Obviously, it is not the text of St. Thomas which is of first interest in this procedure.
35. De Scorraille, I, 251.
36. Cf. *ibid.*, n. 1. De Scorraille remarks that we still have Suárez's original manuscript of this work.
37. In this connection, cf.: "Suarez laissait un certain nombre d'ouvrages tout préparés pour l'impression; mais l'apparition de tel d'entre eux se trouvait différée *sine die* par l'interdiction de rien publier sur le sujet des controverses *de auxiliis*. Les autres, pendant les dix ans qui suivirent la mort de Suarez, furent presque tous édités par le P. Balthazar Alvarès, son collgue et son ami, qui édita aussi les cours que Suarez avait laissés sans pouvoir lui-même en faire la revision." Monnot, *loc. cit.*, cols. 2640-1. On Baltasar Alvarez, cf. C. Sommervogel, *Bibliothèque de la Compagnie de Jésus* (Brussels-Paris,

editions of Suárez's *Opera omnia* published after 1617. The most accessible of these, and the one which I have mainly used for this translation, comprises twenty-six volumes of text, most running close to 1000 pages, in quarto![38] One author, who has "conservatively estimated" Suárez's output at "upwards of twenty-one million words," has gone on to remark:

> this would account for more than two hundred and eighty novels of seventy-five thousand words apiece. Truly a gigantic task for any author, but when we consider that all of Suárez's work was done in the highly precise and technical fields of theology, philosophy, and law, the comparison between him and a modern novelist limps badly. Prolific is a weak adjective to apply to him.[39]

The majority of Suárez's writings are quite naturally of a theological character. This is not to deny their philosophical importance. Indeed, some have had great influence beyond theological circles and concerns. But they usually correspond to some definite area of the *Summa Theologiae* of St. Thomas. Thus, in correlation with the First Part (Ia) of the *Summa* we have the treatises: *De divina substantiae ejusque attributis* ("On the Divine Substance and its Attributes"), *De divino praedestinatione* ("On Divine Predestination"), *De SS. Trinitatis mysterio* ("On the Mystery of the Most Holy Trinity"), all gathered under the title, *De Deo uno et trino* ("On God, One and Triune"), and first published at Coimbra in 1606; and also, *De angelis* ("On the Angels"), *De opere sex dierum* ("On the Work of the Six Days [of Creation]"), and *De Anima* ("On the Soul"), collected under the title, *De Deo effectore creaturarum omnium* ("On God, the Maker of all Creatures") and published posthumously at Lyons in 1620-1621.[40]

---

1890 ff.), Vol. I, cols. 221-222.
38. Cf. Suarez, Franciscus, S.J., *Opera Omnia*, 26 vols. (Paris: L. Vivès, 1856-1866); plus two volumes of indices, 1878. Unless otherwise noted, later references to and citations of Suárez will be from this edition.
39. Fichter, *op. cit.*, 327.
40. De Scorraille, II, 402-403. The beginning of his *De Deo uno et trino* marked a change in Suárez's relation to the text of St. Thomas. This latter is no longer reproduced and commented upon. Instead, he merely gives a table of concordance between St. Thomas and himself or, even less, a simple general reference in the preface of a particular work. Cf. P. Monnot, *loc. cit.*, 2644; see Suárez, *De Deo uno et trino*, Lectori optimi (*Opera omnia*, ed. Vivès, I, xv).

Corresponding to the First Section of the Second Part (Ia IIae) of the *Summa* are the treatises: *De ultimo fine hominis* ("On the Last End of Man"), *De voluntario et involuntario* ("On the Voluntary and the Involuntary"), *De bonitate et malitia actuum humanorum* ("On the Goodness and Evil of Human Acts"), *De vitiis atque peccatis* ("On Vices and Sins"), published together in one volume in Lyons in 1628; and also: *De legibus seu de Deo legislatore* ("On Laws or on God the Legislator"). The fruit of Suárez's teaching at Coimbra between 1601 and 1603, the *De legibus* was edited by its author in 1612 and published that same year also at Coimbra.[41] Additionally here are three volumes, *De Gratia* ("On Grace"), I and III published at Coimbra in 1619 and II at Lyons in 1651. Here too belongs the *De vera intelligentia auxilii efficacis* ("On the True Understanding of [God's] Efficacious Aid"), written in connection with the above mentioned controversy *De auxiliis*, and published at Lyons in 1655. To the Second Section of the Second Part (IIa IIae) correspond: *De fide, spe et caritate* ("On Faith, Hope, and Charity"), Lyons and Coimbra, 1621,[42] and four volumes entitled, *De virtute et statu religionis* ("On the Virtue and State of Religion") of which the first two appeared at Coimbra in 1608 and 1609 and the others at Lyons in 1624 and 1625.[43]

Corresponding to the Third Part (IIIa) of the *Summa* are the already mentioned *De verbo incarnato* and *De mysteriis vitae Christi*, the *De sacramentis* ("On the Sacraments") in two volumes, appearing respectively at Alcalá (1592) and Coimbra (1602), and also one volume, *De censuris* ("On Censures") published at Coimbra in 1603.[44]

---

41. De Scorraille, I, p. xx; II, p. 156. The *De legibus* is contained in Volumes V and VI of the Vivès edition. For a modern critical edition, cf. Francisco Suárez, 1548-1617, *De legibus*. Edición crítica bilingüe por Luciano Pereña [*et al.*], in *Corpus Hispanorum de Pace*, vols. 11, 12, 13, 14, 15, 16, 17, 21, and 22, Madrid, 1971-1981.
42. The treatise "On Faith" was originally composed in 1583 at the Jesuit *Collegium Romanum* as lectures on the opening questions of the *Summa Theologiae* II-II of St. Thomas. This first version was recently edited from four manuscripts and published in three parts. For this, see: Franciscus Suarez, S.J., *Lectiones de Fide, anno 1583 in Collegio Romano habitas*, ad fidem codicum manuscriptorum edidit Carolus Deuringer (Granada, 1967), and "De Fide, Secunda Pars, 1583," ed. del Dr. Karl Deuringer, *Archivo Teológico Granadino*, 32 (1969) pp. 79-232; 33 (1970) pp. 191-305. The *De Fide* itself was revised again for lectures at Coimbra in 1613-1614, Suárez's last year of teaching; cf. Monnot, *loc. cit.*, col. 2647 and De Scorraille, II, 163. Finally, all that the master left was combined and published by Alvarez in the 1621 volume, which also included shorter treatments of hope and charity from the period of Suárez's Roman teaching; *ibid*. The Alvarez text was re-edited by C. Berton in Volume XII (1858) of the Vivès edition. For Alvarez's own rather cryptic comments about its provenance, cf. *ibid.*, pp. vi-vii, 154, 219, 244, and 333.
43. De Scorraille, II, 403; Monnot, 2644-2649.
44. De Scorraille, II, 402-403; Monnot, 2642-2643.

Outside this Thomistic framework are at least two controversial writings: the previously spoken of *De immunitate ecclesiastica a Venetis violata* and the *Defensio fidei catholicae adversus anglicanae sectae errores, cum responsione ad apologiam pro juramento fidelitatis et praefationem monitoriam serenissimi Jacobi Angliae Regis* (literally: "A Defense of the Catholic Faith against the Errors of the Anglican Sect, with a Reply to the 'Apology' for the 'Oath of Fidelity' and the 'Warning Preface' of James, the Most Serene King of England"), which appeared at Coimbra in 1613.[45] In the year of its appearance this latter work was condemned by James I and publicly burned in London, for the reason that in it Suárez had opposed the absolute right of kings and had defended the indirect power of the papacy over temporal rulers, as well as the legitimate resistance of the citizenry against a tyrannical monarch – even to the point of tyrannicide in the case of a monarch deposed for heresy by the pope.[46]

Also outside the Thomistic framework are the two volumes which comprise Suárez's famous *Disputationes metaphysicae* ("Metaphysical Disputations"). Of an explicit philosophical character, this work first saw the light at Salamanca in 1597, when it was published by the brothers Juan and Andrés Renaut under the title, *Metaphysicarum disputationum, in quibus et universa naturalis theologia ordinate traditur, et quaestiones omnes ad duodecim Aristotelis libros pertinentes accurate disputantur . . . Tomus prior – Tomus posterior* ("First [and] Second Tomes of Metaphysical Disputations in which the whole of Natural Theology is treated and all Questions pertaining to [the first] Twelve Books of Aristotle are Disputed"). The two volumes were published at almost the same time. "I hope," said Suárez, "one will not have finished reading the first before the second, whose printing has already begun, will be available."[47]

---

45. The text of this work takes up the whole of Volume XXIV (1859) of the Vivès edition. For critical editions of parts of this work, cf. Francisco Suárez, *Defensio Fidei III. Principatus Politicus o la Soberania popular*, introducción y edición bilingüe por E. Elorduy y L. Pereña (Madrid, 1965) and *De juramento fidelitatis*, edición critica bilingüe por L. Pereña, V. Abril y C. Baciero y la colaboración de A. Garcia y C. Villanueva, in *Corpus Hispanorum de Pace*, Vol. 19 (Madrid, 1978).
46. De Scorraille, II, 165-221, esp. 193; Fichter, pp. 290-303. On the general background of Suárez's controversy with King James, see Francisco Elias de Tejada, "Suárez y el pensamiento inglés contemporaneo," in *Homenaje al Dr. Eximio P. Suárez, S.J., en el IV Centenario de su Nacimiento, 1548-1948*, T. Andrés Marcos et. al. (Salamanca, 1948), pp. 27-43.
47. Cf. *Disputationes metaphysicae* (hereafter *DM*), Ratio . . . ad lectorem; Vivès Vol. XXV. In the thirty-nine years from 1597 to 1636 there appeared seventeen editions of the *Disputationes*. In order, these were at Salamanca (1597), Venice (1599), Mainz (1600), Mainz, Venice, and Paris (1605), Cologne (1608), Venice (1610), Geneva [2 editions], Cologne, and Mainz (1614), Paris and Venice (1619), Cologne (1620), Mainz (1630), and Geneva (1636); for this, cf. J. Iriarte, "La proyección sobre Europa de una gran metafísica – o – Suárez en la filosofía de los dias del Barocco," *Razón y Fe*, número extraordinario (Madrid, 1948), p. 236. Iriarte regards this amazing diffusion of Suárez's

Perhaps the most important enterprise of the *Doctor eximius*, the *Disputationes metaphysicae* is a complete *résumé* of his own and previous Scholastic thought on a myriad of questions, arranged in the form of fifty-four "Disputations" dealing with various topics systematically. Although the questions treated are philosophical and although it was Suárez's intention to restrict his work to such questions,[48] nevertheless, the *Disputationes* are, in the best tradition of medieval thought, meant to be at the service of theology. For this reason and, he says, to foster piety in his readers he has made repeated forays into theological questions – not so much to solve them as to indicate the way in which metaphysical principles may be used to confirm theological truths.[49]

In format, Suárez's *Disputationes* represented a radical departure from previous metaphysical treatises. Until its appearance, metaphysics had been explicitly treated either just incidentally in the form of *Opuscula* ("little works"), such as St. Thomas Aquinas's *De ente et essentia* ("On Being and Essence"), or in commentaries on the text of Aristotle.[50] Both

---

work as perhaps unique in the history of philosophy and compares it with the early editions of Descartes' work: "Descartes, por ejemplo, en todo el siglo XVII alcanzó cuatro ediciones del conjunto total de sus Obras filosóficas. Y de sus 'Meditationes Metafísicas', por separado, en ese mismo siglo (1641-1700), neuve ediciones. Meditaciones que no son sino un folleto, después de todo." *ibid.*, n. 6. On the editions of Suárez's *Disputationes*, see E. M. Rivière, *Suarez et son oeuvre à la occasion du troisième centenaire de sa mort. I: La bibliographie des ouvrages imprimés et inédits* (Toulouse and Barcelona, 1917), p. 14.

48. See *DM*, Ratio... ad lectorem; Vol. XXV.
49. Cf. *ibid.*; see also *DM* 1, proemium (XXV, 1).
50. "The Middle Ages produced a few small purely metaphysical treatises, such as St. Thomas' *De Ente et Essentia*, but Suarez' *Disputationes Metaphysicae* is the first complete and systematic treatise in scholastic metaphysics." Armand A. Maurer, C.S.B., *Medieval Philosophy* (New York, 1962), p. 357; cf. also: "L'importance de Suarez provient justement du fait qu'il a été le premier à ériger un ensemble métaphysique en un temps où l'on ressentait la necessité de disposer d'autre chose que d'une série de commentaires aristotéliciens, ou d'une philosophie rhétoricienne à la Pierre Ramus, ou d'une vague théorie sceptique." J. Ferrater Mora, "Suarez et la philosophie moderne," *Revue de Métaphysique et de Morale*, 68 (1963), p. 59; cf. "Die *Disputationes metaphysicae* des Suarez bedeuten den Uebergang von den Metaphysikkommentaren zu den selbständigen Metaphysiklehrbüchern." Martin Grabmann, "Die *Disputationes Metaphysicae* des Franz Suarez," in *Mittelalterliches Geistesleben*, I (München, 1926), p. 539; ibid., 540 and see 541 for successors to Suárez in this new text book tradition.

Possible forerunners of the *Disputationes* might be the *Sapientiale* of Thomas of York (d. ca. 1260) or the *Summa Philosophiae* formerly attributed to Robert Grosseteste (d. 1253). Information about the first may be found in M. Grabmann, "Die Metaphysik des Thomas von York," *Beiträge zur Geschichte der Philosophie des Mittelalters*, Supplementband I (Münster i. W., 1913), pp. 181-193 and esp. Ephrem Longpré, "Thomas d'York, O.F.M., la première somme métaphysique du XIIIe siècle," *Archivum Franciscanum Historicum*, XIX (1926), pp. 875-920. For a less laudatory comment on this work, see E. Gilson, *History of Christian Philosophy in the Middle Ages* (New York, 1955), p. 665, n. 51. About the *Summa Philosophiae*, see C. K. McKeon, *A Study of the 'Summa Philosophiae' of the Pseudo-Grosseteste* (New York: Columbia University Press, 1948) and E. Gilson, *op. cit.*, pp. 268-273. Yet another forerunner

methods were clearly unsatisfactory, the one incomplete and the other shackled to the rambling obsolete order of Aristotle. So Suárez says that he intends to give, preparatory to theology, a complete exposition of metaphysics which, instead of following the text of Aristotle, will proceed in a systematic fashion.[51]

In executing his intention, the *Doctor eximius* has divided his work into two main parts, to which correspond two tomes. After explaining in the first Disputation the object, the dignity, and the utility of metaphysics, he proceeds in the first part to treat of being in general, its properties and causes. In the second tome, he descends to items under being, considering them from a metaphysical viewpoint.[52]

The first part studies the concept of being (Disputation 2) which, representing in some way everything that entails an order to existence, transcends all genera, species and differences. It will encompass everything real, from extrinsic denominations,[53] through mere possibles,[54] to the subsistent, purely actual, and necessary reality of God. Following this is a treatment of the essential properties of every being inasmuch as it is a being, namely, unity, truth and goodness. Under the discussion of unity, space is given to questions concerning the principle of individuation (Disputation 5),[55] the reality of universal natures (Disputation 6),[56] and the various kinds of distinction (Disputation 7).[57] The discussion of truth (Disputation 8) is balanced by discussion of falsity (Disputation 9) and that of goodness (Disputation 10) by that of evil (Disputation 11).[58] After

---

could be the *Delucidarium metaphysicarum disputationum, in Aristotelis decem et quatuor libros Metaphysicorum*, of Agostino Nifo (d. ca. 1538), which Suárez has on occasion cited. Nifo's work, however, is much more a commentary "per modum quaestionis" on Aristotle's *Metaphysics* than an independent metaphysical synthesis. For Suárez citing Nifo within the 54th Disputation, see translation Section V, n. 3.

51. Cf. *DM*, Ratio ... ad lectorem; XXV; and *DM* 2, prooemium (XXV, 64).
52. See *DM*, Ratio ... ad lectorem; XXV. On abstraction from matter as the touchstone for a metaphysical viewpoint, see *DM* 1, s. 2, n. 22 (XXV, 19).
53. On these, see my article: "Prolegomena to a Study of Extrinsic Denomination in the Work of Francis Suarez, S.J.," *Vivarium*, XXII, 2 (1984), pp. 121-160.
54. Cf. my article: "Suárez and the Reality of the Possibles," *The Modern Schoolman*, XLVI (1967), pp.29-40.
55. For this, see Suárez, Francisco, "Disputatio V: Individual Unity and its Principle," tr. Jorge J. E. Gracia, in *Suárez on Individuation* (Milwaukee: Marquette University Press, 1982).
56. See Suárez, Francisco, *On Formal and Universal Unity*, tr. James F. Ross (Milwaukee: Marquette University Press, 1964).
57. See Suárez, Francisco, *On the Various Kinds of Distinctions*, tr. Cyril Vollert, Milwaukee: Marquette University Press, 1947.
58. Cf. Jorge J. E. Gracia and Douglas Davis, *The Metaphysics of Good and Evil according to Suárez: Metaphysical Disputations X and XI and Selected Passages from Disputation XXII and Other Works*, Translation with Introduction, Notes, and Glossary (München: Philosophia Verlag, 1989).

the essential properties, there follows a consideration of the causes of being. Disputation 12 treats causes in general while Disputations 13-25 deal with various types of causes. Concluding this first part, Disputation 26 presents a comparison of causes with their effects and Disputation 27 considers the mutual relations of causes one to another.

The second part opens with the division of being into infinite and finite (Disputation 28). Infinite being, or God, is the subject of the next two Disputations. In Disputation 29, the existence and unicity of God is demonstrated *metaphysically*.[59] Disputation 30 goes on to investigate, as far as unaided human reason can, the divine perfection, simplicity, immensity, immutability, wisdom, and omnipotence. With Disputation 31 Suárez begins his treatment of finite being. It is this Disputation which is the locus of the famed Suarezian denial of the real distinction between essence and existence in creatures.[60] In Disputation 32, Suárez considers the distinction of substance and accident in general. Substance is treated in metaphysical detail through the next four Disputations while the different categories of accident are the subject matter of Disputations 37 to 53. The fifty-fourth Disputation, which is our special concern, concludes the whole work with a discussion of "beings of reason" including negations, privations, and reason-dependent relations – all of which fall outside real being, the object of metaphysics.[61]

The most superficial reader of Suárez's *Disputationes* must be impressed by their tremendous display of their author's learning. Throughout the two volumes, after stating each problem, the *Doctor eximius* resorts to the history of philosophy and theology in search of solutions which have been offered for it. The integrity of his research is almost incredible. It seems every conceivable Greek, Patristic, and especially Scholastic writer is cited one or more times. As many as twenty-two

---

59. On this, see my article "The Suarezian Proof for God's Existence," in *History of Philosophy in the Making: A Symposium of Essays to Honor Professor James D. Collins on his 65th Birthday*, ed. Linus J. Thro (Washington, D.C., 1982), pp. 105-117. Also cf., Joseph Owens, C.SS.R., "The Conclusion of the *Prima Via*," *The Modern Schoolman*, 30 (1952-53), 33-53, 109-121, 203-215.
60. For this, see Francis Suárez, *On the Essence of Finite Being as Such, on the Existence of that Essence and their Distinction*, translated from the Latin with an Introduction by Norman J. Wells, (Milwaukee: Marquette University Press, 1983). Also cf.: J. Owens, "The Number of Terms in the Suarezian Discussion of Essence and Being," *The Modern Schoolman*, XXXIV (1957), 147-191; N. J. Wells, "Suárez, Historian and Critic of the Modal Distinction between Essential Being and Existential Being," *The New Scholasticism*, XXXVI (1962), 419-444; J. Gómez Caffarena, "Sentido de la composición de ser y esencia en Suárez," *Pensamiento*, XV (1969), 135-154.
61. On the restriction of metaphysics to real being, exclusive of beings of reason, cf. *DM* 1, s.1, n. 26 (XXV, 11).

opinions have been listed with respect to a single question.[62] Normally, these opinions are cited from the original source[63] and a reference is given. One historian has compiled a list of 7709 of these citations and has found 245 different authors mentioned.[64] Among these Aristotle was most frequently cited, in all a total of 1735 times, while St. Thomas Aquinas was next, receiving the nod 1008 times.[65] The complete list includes not merely great writers and principal representatives of philosophic schools

---

62. For this, see Hunter Guthrie, S.J., "The Metaphysics of Francis Suarez," *Thought*, XVI (1941), 301.
63. "The habit of quoting from the numerous collections of citations and abridged texts known as *Catenae aureae*, which contained many inaccuracies and were far from complete, was abandoned for the more scholarly practice of quoting and summarizing from the original text itself." Guthrie, *loc. cit.*, 303. This opinion of Guthrie may be a little exaggerated. However, considering those authors most quoted and their ratio to the overall number of quotations, I would say that "normally" Suárez cites from original texts. For a less laudatory estimate of Suárez's citations, see N. J. Wells, "Suárez, Historian...," esp. 443.
64. See J. Iturrioz, S.J., "Fuentes de la metafísica de Suárez," *Pensamiento*, número extraordinario (Madrid, 1948), p. 39.
65. Cf. *ibid.*, p. 40. In this place Iturrioz gives us the following table of authors cited more than thirty times each:

1. Aristotle: 1,735
2. S. Thomas: 1,008
3. Suárez: 971
4. Scotus: 363
5. S. Augustine: 334
6. Cajetan: 299
7. Soncinas: 192
8. Averroes: 179
9. Durandus: 153
10. Syl. of Ferrara: 124
11. S. Greg. Nazian.: 117
12. Capreolus: 115
13. P. Fonseca: 114
14. C. Javellus: 97
15. S. Albert the Great: 96
16. Henry of Ghent: 95
17. Plato: 92
18. G. Biel: 86
19. Avicenna: 84
20. Aegidius: 78
21. Hervaeus: 77
22. Soto: 75
23. Alex. of Hales: 71
24. S. John Damascene: 71
25. Wm. of Ockham: 67
26. Ps. Dionysius: 56
27. Alex. of Aphrodisias: 52
28. P. Aureoli: 46
29. Simplicius: 41
30. Anton. Andreas: 40
31. S. Bonaventure: 38
32. Marsilius of Inghen: 37
33. S. Anselm: 36
34. Rich. of Middleton: 35
35. Boethius: 33

Among other things, in this table note Suárez's cross-references to himself, his citation of Averroes much more than Avicenna, and his comparatively few citations of the nominalists, Gabriel Biel and William of Ockham. This last is interesting in view of the accusation of nominalism which has been made against Suárez; e.g. see L. Mahieu, *François Suarez, sa philosophie et les rapports qu'elle a avec sa théologie* (Paris, 1921), 288, 499, 501, 504, 505, and 522; also J. Maréchal, *Le point de départ de la Métaphysique*, Vol. I (Paris, 1923), p. 185. For reply to the accusation, see Pedro Descoqs, S.J., "Thomisme et Suarézisme," *Archives de Philosophie*, IV (1926), 82-192 and J. M. Alejandro, S.J., *La gnoseología del Doctor Eximio y la acusación nominalista* (Comillas, 1948), esp. pp. 375-376, where there are listed citations by Suárez of Ockham and his nominalist successors.

but also their commentators and little known disciples.[66] Since such relatively minor figures often reveal trends or give astute interpretations of their masters, their opinions are still of interest for the historian of philosophy.[67] Again, because many of their works have become rare, their representation in Suárez's pages gains added importance. This is enhanced by the fact that Suárez is "supremely apt at summing up a case,"[68] seldom dodges an issue, and gives due weight to every position including those of his adversaries. Indeed, if he has a fault as an historian it lies in his passion for equity.[69]

Most certainly, Suárez himself was affected by his own erudition. Again and again his pages reveal his dependence upon his predecessors and contemporaries alike, for both statements of philosophical problems and their solutions. This is not to take anything away, since every philosopher who ever wrote, with the possible exception of Thales, has depended on those who went before.[70] The lines of Suárez's dependence with respect to beings of reason are of interest to us and, in what follows, I have tried to note at least some of them.

As for his own place in the history of philosophy – through his writings Suárez exercised wide influence on post-Renaissance, especially 17th century, Scholasticism. Largely through the growth and agency of the Jesuit order, Suárez's metaphysics spread from the Catholic schools of Spain and Portugal to various northern European locales.[71] In particular,

---

66. For example, it contains such figures as Dominic of Flanders, O.P. (d. 1479), who is cited 11 times, Peter of La Palu, O.P. (d. 1342), cited 10 times, and Francis Lychetus, O.F.M. (d. 1520), who is mentioned 10 times.
67. For example, cf. E. Gilson's remark on Lychetus: "The commentary of Lychetus on the *Opus Oxoniense* is an excellent guide to the study of Scotism." *History of Christian Philosophy* . . . , p. 800, n. 77.
68. E. Gilson, *Being and Some Philosophers* (Toronto, 1952), p. 99.
69. In Gilson's view, Suárez is "unfortunately, so anxious not to hurt equity that a moderate verdict is most likely to be considered a true verdict. Rather than judge, Suárez arbitrates, with the consequence that he never wanders very far from the truth and frequently hits upon it, but, out of pure moderation of mind, sometimes contents himself with a 'near miss'." *ibid.* For a view of Suárez as an historian which is in part contrary to that of Gilson, cf. Norman J. Wells, "Suarez, Historian and Critic of the Modal Distinction between Essential Being and Existential Being," *The New Scholasticism*, XXXVI (1962), 419-444, esp. 443.
70. I am thinking here of Prof. Wolfson's remark, "that philosophers, after all, see the universe which they try to explain as already interpreted to them in books, with the only possible exception perhaps of the first recorded philosopher, and all he could see was water." Harry Austryn Wolfson, *The Philosophy of Spinoza* (New York: Meridian Books, 1958), Vol. 1, p. 3.
71. Cf. "Les Disputationes Metaphysicae de Suarez ont exercé une vaste influence sur la méditation et l'enseignement philosophique en Europe. Leur rayonnement fut servi par la dispersion des philosophes jésuites qui s'installaient à Ingolstadt, Vienne, Wurtzbourg, Mayence, Prague, Trèves, Cologne, Fribourg en Brisgau." J. F. Mora, *loc. cit.*, p. 62. On the northern expansion of the Jesuits, see Bernhard Duhr, *Geschichte der Jesuiten in den Ländern deutscher Zunge*, Vols. I and II (Freiburg im B., 1907-1913).

it penetrated the Protestant universities of Germany where the *Disputationes metaphysicae* was pondered especially by those who favored Melanchthon's rather than Luther's attitude toward philosophy.[72] Indeed, in a number of 17th and 18th century German universities it served as a textbook in philosophy.[73] In much the same way, Suárez had major influence in Dutch Protestant schools[74] both in metaphysics[75] and also in law, including international law. To sense Suárez's importance here for the provenance of modern international law, it is enough to recall that, for the famous Dutch jurisprudent, Hugo Grotius (1583-1645), our Jesuit doctor was a philosopher and theologian of such penetration "that he hardly had an equal."[76]

Beyond this, as Martin Heidegger would later see it, Suárez was the main source through which Greek ontology passed from the middle ages to usher in the 'metaphysics' and the transcendental philosophy of modern times.[77] More than likely, Suarezian metaphysics was that first learned by Descartes from his Jesuit teachers at La Flèche.[78] – On occasion he has mentioned the *Disputationes*,[79] of which he is believed to have

---

Also, cf. C. Noreña, "Suárez and the Jesuits," esp. 269-270.

72. For this, see J. Iriarte, "La proyección sobre Europa de una gran metafísica - o - Suárez en la filosofía de los dias del Barocco," *Razón y fe*, número extraordinario (Madrid, 1948), pp. 229-265, esp. p. 236; also: Ernst Lewalter, *Spanische-jesuitische und deutschlutherische Metaphysik des 17 Jahrhunderts* (Hamburg, 1935); Karl Eschweiler, "Die Philosophie der spanischen Spätscholastik auf der Universitäten des 17 Jahrhunderts," in *Spanische Forschungen der Görresgesellschaft* (Münster i. W., 1928), pp. 251-325; Max Wundt, *Die deutsche Schulmetaphysik des 17 Jahrhunderts* (Tübingen, 1939).

73. Cf. "A l'exception de celle d'Altdorf, presque toutes les Universités de l'Europe centrale adoptent alors la tradition hispano-portuguise pour base de l'enseignement et de la systematisation de la métaphysique." J. F. Mora, *loc. cit.*, pp. 63-64.

74. Cf. F. Sassen, "La influencia de Suárez en las universidades protestantes de los Paises Bajos en los siglos XVII y XVIII" (resumen de la communicación), *Congreso Internacional de Filosofía, Barcelona, 4-10 Octubre 1948*, III (Madrid, 1949), 471.

75. For much of this, see Paul Dibon, *La philosophie néerlandaise au siècle d'or*, Tome I (Paris, Amsterdam, etc., 1954).

76. Cf. Grotius, *Epist.* CLIV, Joanni Cordesio, 15 Oct. 1633, as cited by De Scorraille, *op. cit.*, II, p 437. For some of Suárez's influence on Grotius as well as on international law generally, cf. J. Larequi, S.J., "Influencia suareciana en la filosofía de Grocio," *Razón y Fe*, 88 (1929), pp. 525-538; Isidoro Ruiz Moreno, "El derecho internacional y Francisco Suárez," in *Actas del IV Centenario del Nacimiento de Francisco Suárez (1548-1948)* (Burgos, 1949), II, pp. 331-363; also Teodoro Andrés Marcos, "El supernacionalismo de Suárez, en su tratado 'De Legibus' Lib. II," Cap. XVII-XX, *ibid.*, pp. 367-386.

77. For Heidegger, see *Sein und Zeit* (Halle, 1941), p. 22, tr. McQuarrie and Robinson, *Being and Time* (New York, 1962), p. 43; also cf.: *Die Frage nach dem Ding* (Tübingen, 1962), p. 77. For at least part of what is involved here, see my article, "Heidegger and Scholastic Metaphysics," *The Modern Schoolman*, XLIX (1972), pp. 201-220.

78. Cf. Gilson, *Being* . . . , p. 109.

79. Cf. Descartes, *Reply to the Fourth Objections*, where he cites Suárez, *DM* 9, 2, 4; in *Oeuvres de Descartes*, ed. Adam-Tannery (1897 sq.), VII, 235; also see Leonard Gilen, S.J., "Ueber die Beziehungen Descartes' zur zeitgenössichen Scholastik," *Scholastik*, XXXII (1957), esp. p. 54, n. 71.

owned a copy.[80] At the same time, among modern historians there is some disagreement about how well he really knew the work.[81]

About Leibniz there is less quarrel. He himself boasted that while yet a youth he had read Suárez "like a novel."[82] Schopenhauer, too, in his chief work, *Die Welt als Wille und Vorstellung*, shows himself very well acquainted with the *Disputationes*,[83] which he values as "a true compendium of Scholasticism" and "an authentic compendium of the whole Scholastic tradition."[84] But, perhaps most striking, is the fact that for Christian Wolff it was clearly "Francisco Suárez, of the Society of Jesus, who among Scholastics pondered metaphysical questions with particular penetration."[85] Moreover, in the construction of his own *Ontologia*, a

---

80. Gilson, *Being* . . . , p. 109.
81. According to A. Maurer (*op. cit.*, p. 336), Descartes "acquired a firsthand knowledge of Suarez' most important work, the *Disputationes Metaphysicae*." Somewhat less appreciative of Descartes' knowledge of the *Disputationes* is F. Copleston, S.J. (*A History of Philosophy*, III, p. 378): ". . . apparently, he did not know it well at all." Cf.: "Himself a pupil of the Jesuits, he had learned metaphysics according to Suarez, and, though I would not bet that he had read the whole *Metaphysicae Disputationes*, there are positive reasons to feel sure that he knew the work, and I even believe that, for a time at least, he personally owned a copy of it." E. Gilson, *Being* . . . , p. 109; and also "Als sicher muss angenommen werden, dass Descartes auch schon in La Flèche die später von ihm benützten und ausdrücklich zitierten *Disputationes metaphysicae* des Suarez kannte und konsultierte." L. Gilen, *op. cit.*, p. 47. On the probable influence of Suárez's being of reason doctrine on Descartes, cf. Antonio Millán-Puelles, *Teoría del objeto puro* (Madrid, 1990), pp. 465-6.
82. See *Vita Leibnitii a seipso*, in Foucher de Careil, *Nouvelles lettres et opuscles inédits de Leibniz* (Paris, 1857), p. 382-383; as cited by L. Mahieu, *op. cit.*, p. 517-518. Also cf. P. Mesnard, "Comment Leibniz se trouva placé dans le sillage de Suarez," *Archives de Philosophie*, XVIII, cahier 1 (Paris, 1949), pp. 7-32; Mesnard (esp. pp. 22-30) has much of interest to say about Suárez's *Disputationes* in the Protestant universities of Germany. On a particular point, cf.: "Más elocuente todavia es el caso de Leibniz que se licencia en Leipzig con al tesis 'Del Principio de individuación,' siendo profesor Thomasio (J.). Un trabajo que no sólo delata influjos de Suárez sino que es continuación de su Disputatio 5, en la se apartó el de los escotistas, tomistas y nominalistas. 'Pono ergo omne individuum tota sua entitate individuatum,' es la posición de Suárez-leibniz." J. Iriarte, *loc. cit.*, 248-249. For a contrary opinion, cf. Jean François Courtine (*Suarez et le système de la métaphysique* (Paris, 1990) who (pp. 446-519) discounts the influence of Suárez on Leibniz's 1663 *Disputatio metaphysica de principio individui* ("Metaphysical Disputation on the Principle of the Individual") and regards Leibniz as closer in this to the nominalists than to Suárez.
83. Cf. *Arthur Schopenhauers sämtliche Werke*, ed. P. Deussen, I (München, 1911), 134, 148, 181, 500; cited by N. Junk, *Die Bewegungslehre des Franz Suarez* (Innsbruck, Leipzig, 1938), p. 13; also see M. Grabmann, *loc. cit.*, 535.
84. Cf. "diesem wahrem Kompendio der Scholastik"; "diesem echten Kompendio der ganzen scholastischen Weisheit." A. Schopenhauer, *Sämtliche Werke*, ed. Griesbach, III, 20; IV, 70; as cited by M. Grabmann, *loc. cit.*, p. 535.
85. "Sane Franciscus Suarez e Societate Jesu, quem inter Scholasticos res metaphysicas profundius meditatum esse constat . . . ." C. Wolff, *Philosophia prima sive ontologia*, I, 2, 3, n. 169 (Francofurti et Lipsiae, 1736), p. 138.

work which for Immanuel Kant was practically co-terminous with pre-Critical metaphysics,[86] Wolff was very much a debtor to Suárez.[87]

But beyond all this, a fuller story of Suárez's influence on the philosophy of the 17th century and after remains to be told. And I am certain that when it is told, it will especially include Suárez's role in the development of intentionality theory among his Jesuit successors. It will also I think include his working through them to inspire many thinkers leading up to Kant. Someday soon I hope to tell more of this story. But for now I am content to put a first foundation in place with this translation of his 54th Disputation.

---

86. "To innumerable professors and students of philosophy, metaphysics was Wolff and what Wolff had said was metaphysics. To Immanuel Kant, in particular, it never was to be anything else, so that the whole Critique of Pure Reason ultimately rests upon the assumption that the bankruptcy of the metaphysics of Wolff had been the very bankruptcy of metaphysics." Gilson, *Being* ..., p. 119.
87. Cf. *ibid*., pp. 112-120.

## II. Introduction to the 54th Disputation.

### A. The Setting:

The 54th Disputation was important in Suárez's own mind inasmuch as it set limits for the science of metaphysics and even confronted the limits of what is thinkable and sayable.[1] In this Disputation, Suárez passed from "being insofar as it is real being"[2] or "being insofar as it is actual or possible" (which he identified as the subject or object of metaphysics)[3] to consider "beings" which do not or even cannot exist despite the fact that we can think and speak of them with truth and meaning.

That truth and meaning are functions of being has been a commonplace in the Western philosophical tradition from Parmenides (fl. ca. 485 B.C.) on.[4] One need only remember the Platonic doctrine of Forms, which were at once "beingly being" (τὸ ὄντως ὄν) and the locus of intelligibility and truth. At the same time, Plato in the *Theatetus* and again in the *Sophist* raised problems with respect to non-existing things. In the *Theatetus*, considering the difference between true and false belief, Socrates rejected the view that false belief is directed toward that which is not, on the ground that to think what is not is to think nothing, which is not to think at all.[5] The issue recurred in the *Sophist*, where it was stated

---

1. For much of this Introduction, I will be drawing on articles which I have previously published. In chronological order, these are principally: "Prolegomena to a Study of Extrinsic Denomination in the Work of Francis Suarez, S.J.," *Vivarium*, XXII, 2 (1984), pp. 121-160; "Suarez on Beings of Reason and Truth (1)," *Vivarium*, XXV, 1 (1987), pp. 47-75; "Suarez on Beings of Reason and Truth (2)," *Vivarium*, XXVI, 1 (1988), pp. 51-72; "'Extrinsic Cognoscibility': A Seventeenth Century Supertranscendental Notion," *The Modern Schoolman*, LXVIII, 1 (November, 1990), pp. 57-80.
2. For what "real being" involves here, see my article, "Suárez on the Reality of the Possibles," *The Modern Schoolman*, XLV (1967), pp. 29-40.
3. Cf. *DM* 1, s. 1, n. 26 (XXV, p. 11). Suárez frequently uses the words "subject" and "object" synonymously in this context of what is treated by a science; cf. also, e.g., *DM* 1, prol. (XXV, 2); *DM* 2, prol. (64). However, at times and in other contexts, he does distinguish between them; cf., e.g., *DM* 2, 2, n. 25 (XXV, 78); *DM* 6, 3, n. 12 (215); *DM* 31, 2, n. 8 (XXVI, 231); *ibid.*, 3, n. 3 (233); *DM* 54, 2, n. 1 (1018); for this last, see translation *Section* 2, number 1.
4. For this, cf., e.g., τὸ γὰρ αὐτὸ νοεῖν ἐστίν τε καὶ εἶναι (fr. 3); χρὴ τὸ λέγειν τε νοεῖν τ' ἐὸν ἔμμεναι (fr. 6); and ταὐτὸν δ' ἐστι νοεῖν τε καὶ οὕνεκεν ἐστι νόημα. οὐ γὰρ ἄνευ τοῦ ἐόντος, ἐν ᾧ πεφατισμένον ἐστίν εὑρήσεις τὸ νοεῖν. (fr. 8).
5. Cf. *Theatetus* 189 A, B.

that it is false to attribute being to that which is not.[6] Later in the same dialogue the problem was solved to Plato's satisfaction by the theory of the Form of the Other.[7]

While rejecting Plato's Forms, Aristotle himself said or implied that each thing is sayable, intelligible or true to the degree that it has being.[8] Still, Aristotle included privations, negations, and even "nothing" itself among items which were in different ways said to be.[9] At the same time, he apparently excluded them from metaphysical consideration inasmuch as they fall under what he designated "being as true."[10] Connected with this, he shifted emphasis from things themselves to the mind. Better said, for Aristotle truth was found primarily, if not exclusively, in the second operation of the mind – that is, in the judgment by which we combine or separate items which we have first apprehended singly.[11] Thus truth occurs in our judgment that something is which in fact is, or that something is not which in fact is not.[12] Accordingly, truth seems to require at least two things: (1) some mental composition or separation, and (2) a conformity between this and things as they are in themselves.

While not explicitly raising a further problem, Aristotle has occasioned one here in connection with "the goat-stag" (ὁ τραγέλαφος).[13]

---

6. Cf. *Sophist* 238 C; also cf.: – Any statement must be about something rather than nothing, *Sophist* 262 E; – and a false statement speaks about non-beings as though they were beings, *ibid*. 263 B.
7. Cf. *Sophist* 257B - 263B. On all of this, see F. M. Cornford, *Plato's Theory of Knowledge*, reprint of original [1934] edition (Indianapolis: Bobbs-Merrill, 1957), pp. 114-120, 212-214, 289-320. Also cf. L. M. de Rijk, "On Ancient and Mediaeval Semantics and Metaphysics (4, 5, and 6)," *Vivarium*, XIX (1981), pp. 1-46 and 81-125, XX (1982), 97-127; idem, *Plato's Sophist: A Philosophical Commentary* (Amsterdam, 1986), pp. 82-92, 164-185, and 302-305.
8. See, e.g., *Metaphysics* II, c. 1; 993b 30-31. This indeed seems to be the basic thought which animates his doctrine of ten categories, irreducible to one another; cf. "Supponendo, come si deve supporre, che l'intelletto, se non erra, dica ciò che è e non ciò che non è, parlare di modi di dire è la stessa cosa che parlare di modi di eśsere, e i modi di essere si possono chiamare enti. Se dieci quindi sono i diversi predicati, i modi di dire, le categorie (κατηγορέω = affermo, predico), dieci sono le classi degli enti. Questa è certo l'opinione di Aristotele, ..." Carlo Giacon, S.J., *Il devenire in Aristotele* (Padova, 1947), p. 56. With this, compare Suárez, *Translation, Section* V, n. 20: "Indeed, whatever we apprehend in the manner of a positive being must be conceived by analogy or proportion with a being of some real category."
9. Cf. *Metaphysics* IV, c. 2, 1003b 6-11. Note, however, in *Metaphysics* VII, c. 4, 1030a 25-26, he takes this to mean that one can say that non-being is non-being, but not that non-being is without qualification (ἁπλῶς).
10. See *Metaphysics* VI, c. 4, 1027b 34-1028a 3; *ibid*., XI, c. 8, 1065a 22 ff.
11. Cf. *Ibid*. VI, c. 4; 1027b 18ff.
12. Cf. *ibid*. IV, c. 7; 1011b 27.
13. Cf. *Perihermeneias* c. 1, 16a 16. See also: *Prior Analytics* I, c. 38, 49a 24; *Posterior Analytics* II, c. 7, 92b 7-8; *Physics* IV, c. 1, 208a 30.

Mentioned by Plato in the *Republic* (488 A), the goat-stag is a creature of artful imagination, which involves a seemingly impossible synthesis of two essences. Aristotle accepts this, but other questions will arise about the being and intelligibility of such a creature. A goat-stag has no being or intelligibility in itself apart from thought.[14] Moreover, the mental composition which it involves does not suffice for truth.[15] It seems, indeed, just the opposite: *the self-contradictory composition of the goat-stag*[16] makes it a perfect example of what Aristotle has called a "false thing" (πρᾶγμα ψεῦδος ).[17] Paradoxically, however, Aristotle has also declared that the (term) *goat-stag* does have signification.[18] The obvious question is what does it signify? Then, if this has no being or intelligibility as such, what truth can there be in any statements about it?[19] Added questions concern its relation to the being which is said in many ways and to the subject matter of metaphysics.

In the Middle Ages, St. Thomas Aquinas and other Scholastic doctors continued the tradition of the Greeks. Thus for Aquinas, being and truth were convertible (*ens et verum convertuntur*).[20] Being alone was of itself intelligible. There was no basis in non-being for its becoming known. The one way in fact in which it could be known was if the intellect itself were to render it knowable. In this, non-being would become a kind of "being of reason" (*ens rationis*).[21]

In his 54th Disputation, Suárez has reopened the discussion. The mind-dependent "beings of reason" which form the subject matter of the Disputation, while certainly not restricted to impossible things, will at their core be best exemplified by such. Following earlier Scholastics,

---

14. Cf. *Posterior Analytics* II, c. 7, 92b 6. Note that in *Prior Analytics* I, c. 38, 49a 24, Aristotle does say that the goat-stag is knowable in the sense that it can be known not to exist; on this, cf. W. D Ross, *Aristotle's Prior and Posterior Analytics* (Oxford, 1965), p. 410.
15. Cf. *Perihermeneias* c. 1; 16a 16.
16. This is to say if something is a goat, it cannot be a stag and, vice-versa, if something is a stag, that precludes its being a goat.
17. Cf. *Metaphysics* V, c. 29; 1024b 17-18.
18. Cf. *Perihermeneias* c. 1; 16a 16. One may note the evident entry point here for semiotic considerations.
19. The problem may be easily inferred from *Metaphysics* V, c. 7; 1011b 26.
20. Cf. *In Aristotelis libros Peri Hermeneias*, I, l. 3; ed. Spiazzi (Taurini, 1955), n. 27.
21. Cf. "Non-being has nothing in itself whereby it can be known; but it is known in so far as the intellect renders it knowable. Hence the true is based on being, inasmuch as non-being is a certain logical being, apprehended, that is, by reason." ["Ad secundum dicendum quod non ens non habet in se unde cognoscatur, sed cognoscitur inquantum intellectus facit illud cognoscibile. Unde verum fundatur in ente, inquantum non ens est quoddam *ens rationis*, apprehensum scilicet a ratione. (emphasis added)]" *Summa Theologiae* I, q. 16, art. 3, ad 2; tr. Anton C. Pegis, in *Introduction to St. Thomas Aquinas* (New York, 1948), p. 173.

Suárez here will consider the goat-stag (in Latin the *hircocervus*)[22] and other items which have no being outside the mind but which are yet in some way intelligible. In so doing he will present the most detailed and systematic treatment of "beings of reason" up to his time. This treatment will provide for these beings a taxonomy which will form the basis for nuanced meditations on their meaning and truth and which will dominate discussions of them for at least a century after. At times along the way, a modern reader may sense Suárez's almost Kant-like concern for objectivity and feel him close even to our own century's interests in Meinongian entities and Russell's "bald present king of France."[23]

## B. The Prologue and Division of the Disputation:

In a brief prologue to his 54th Disputation, the *Doctor Eximius* notes that beings of reason are not real beings and that they are thus excluded from the direct and proper object of metaphysics. Along with this, however, he remarks how necessary their study is and offers some justification for their inclusion in his metaphysical work.[24] Of interest here is his assessment of them as "not true beings, but as quasi-shadows of being." As such, they have no intrinsic intelligibility, but must be known only indirectly through other things. Immediately flowing from this is the fact that they, like Meinong's later "homeless objects,"[25] are not of direct and primary concern for any science.

All the same, inasmuch as beings of reason are of use in a variety of sciences, they can be grasped and must be treated in some way. In fact, Suárez believes, their treatment is exclusively the concern of the

---

22. See translation, *Section 5*, n. 16.
23. For Russell in reaction to Meinong, cf. B. Russell: "Meinong's Theory of Complexes and Assumptions," *Mind*, NS, XIII (1904), pp. 204-219, 336-354, 509-524; "On Denoting," *ibid.*, NS, XIV (1905), 479-493; "Critical Notice: *Untersuchungen zur Gegenstandstheorie und Psychologie. Mit Unterstützung des k.k. Ministeriums für Kultur und Unterricht in Wien herausgegeben von A. Meinong* (Leipzig: Verlag von Johann Ambrosius Barth, 1904), pp. xi, 634." *ibid.*, pp. 530-538.
24. For this exclusion and justification, see also *DM* 1, s. 1, n. 6; XXV, 3-4. For Aristotle's earlier exclusion of "being as true" from the concern of metaphysics, cf. note 10, above.
25. For this, see A. Meinong, *Ueber die Stellung der Gegenstandstheorie im System der Wissenschaften* (Leipzig, 1907), pp. 8-27 and "Zur Gegenstandstheorie" in *Die Philosophie der Gegenwart in Selbstsdarstellungen* (Leipzig, 1923), translated as Appendix I, "Meinong's Ontology," by Reinhardt Grossmann, in *Meinong* (London, 1974), pp. 224-229. Also cf. Roderick M. Chisholm, *Brentano and Meinong Studies* (Atlantic Highlands, NJ, 1982), "Homeless Objects," pp. 37-52.

metaphysician. For, even though beings of reason have no true being, they are, as mentioned, "shadows" of being. Like being then they have what he calls a "quasi-transcendentality,"[26] which by itself would remove them from the province of any science other than metaphysics. It is true that more particular disciplines, such as physics or logic, sometimes treat certain beings of reason (e.g., privation, the void, or second intentions such as species or genus) in connection with their proper scientific objects. But only metaphysics is wide enough to consider, albeit obliquely and concomitantly with its proper object, the whole range of beings of reason as such.

After the *Prologue*, the Disputation splits into six *Sections*. Of these, the first two treat the existence, the nature, and the causes of beings of reason. *Sections* 3 and 4 consider how such beings of reason are divided. As Suárez sees it, the traditional listing of negations, privations, and relations of reason will exhaust the types that divide beings of reason. *Section* 5 will then more closely examine negations and privations and *Section* 6 will go on to treat relations of reason.

## C. Section I:

Suárez's position on the existence of beings of reason stands midway between two extremes. There are those, such as the Scotist, Francis of Mayronnes (d. ca. 1325), who have denied this existence. Their arguments are at least three. First, if such beings of reason exist as inhering in the mind or as products of the mind, they will hardly be distinguishable from certain real beings, say, intelligible species and concepts, which exist in similar ways. Second, if they are distinguishable from real beings they will be non-real fabrications, which is to say mere nothings lacking all existence and by implication unworthy of, or even impervious to, any serious consideration. Third, the proponents of this view deny that beings of reason are needed for teaching about or conceiving real things. In sum,

---

26. Suárez's frequent employment of the prefix "quasi" is worth noting. Thus in the sections to follow, he will speak of "quasi-essence," "quasi-essential features," "quasi-essential foundation," "quasi-disposition," "quasi-difference," "quasi-passion," and a "quasi-material" cause of beings of reason (as well as imply quasi-formal and quasi-efficient causes for them). Again, he will speak of "quasi-induction" as well as "quasi-intrinsic," "quasi-extrinsic," and "quasi-common" characteristics in their regard. Without pushing it, I cannot help but think of Meinong (in *Ueber Annahmen* [Leipzig, 1910]), speaking of *Quasi-Transzendenz* (220, 228), *Quasi-Wirklichkeit* (224, 226, 263-4, 266), *Quasibedeutung* (59), *Quasiinhalt* (264, 277, 286, 312), etc.

they argue, beings of reason do not exist and there is no need for their existence (I, 2).[27]

The other extreme is represented by those who affirm that beings of reason exist but also affirm that they fall under a concept common to them and to real beings. This last will be especially evident, some Thomistic authors[28] think, between real relations and relations solely dependent on reason (I, 3).[29] Suárez rejects this view of relations as well as the more general view, which it presupposes or implies, of a community of concept between real beings and beings of reason (*ibid.*).

His own position then is that beings of reason do indeed exist. But, most important for the issue of their truth and intelligibility, they do not share a common concept with real being (I, 4). Instead, between beings of reason and real being only the word "being" is common (I, 9).[30] To clarify this, he tells us more exactly just how he is using the term "being of reason." While this term may designate various things, in the present context it is restricted to items which are completely mind-dependent inasmuch as *they exist only objectively in the intellect* (I, 6). That is to say, their whole reality consists in being objects of understanding. This is wide enough to encompass things which we can think but which as such do not, or even cannot ever, actually exist. Examples may be blindness, certain relations of reason, and *most of all* impossible things such as chimerae[31] or goat-

---

27. For a modern denial of beings of reason, such as "nothing" and "evil" and a rejection of what are deemed "pseudo-problems" occasioned by these, cf. Henri Bergson, *Creative Evolution*, tr. A. Mitchell (New York: Random House, 1944), pp. 299-324 and *The Two Sources of Morality and Religion*, tr. R. A. Audra and C. Brereton (New York: Doubleday, 1935), esp. 261-262.
28. Suárez in one place (*DM* 47, 3, n. 2 [XXVI, 794]) has named Cajetan, Capreolus, Deza, Ferrara, and Soncinas.
29. For example, cf. Cajetan commenting on *Summa Theologiae* I, q. 28, art. 1: "Relation is the sort of being for which the qualification existing in the mind does not detract from what is proper to it, as it does detract from what is proper to all other sorts of being. For a rose formed by thought is not a rose, nor is Homer in the mind's consideration Homer; but a relation formed by the mind is a true relation. . . .," as translated in *Tractatus de Signis: The Semiotic of John Poinsot*, Interpretative Arrangement by John N. Deely in consultation with Ralph Austin Powell (Berkeley, 1985), p. 96, n. 18. Deely has rightly seen that this view of relation will become central to the semiotic theory of John Poinsot (a.k.a. John of St. Thomas); cf. *ibid.*, esp. pp. 472-479.
30. Cf. *DM* 4, 8, n. 4 (XXV, 138); *DM* 45, 4, n. 9 (XXVI, 750-1); and Suárez, *Tractatus de Anima*, IV, c. 2, n. 4 (III, 714)
31. Among 16th and 17th century authors, there was not total agreement about the composition of a chimera. Thus, e.g., Domingo Soto, O.P. (1494-1560), relying on Ovid, says it is made up of the head of a lion, the tail of a serpent, and the back of a goat, cf. *Summulae Summularum*, I, c. 7, arg. 3. (Salamancae, 1554), p. 12r.; for the same, see the Conimbricenses: *Commentarii Collegii Conimbricensis S.J. In universam Dialecticam Aristotelis* (ed. Lugduni, 1607), *in praef. Porphyrii*, q. 6, a. 1, (p. 144). But George de Rhodes, S.J. (1597-1661) speaks of it as: (1) a combination of an ox, a lion, and a goat (*Philosophia peripatetica* [Lugduni, 1671], I, d. 2, s. 2, [p. 16]), and (2) a combination of a goat, a lion, and a dragon (*ibid.* [p. 17]).

stags (I, 7). Between such things and real beings, which are the concern of metaphysics, only a name is common. The immediate upshot of this is that beings of reason are not subsumed under the Suarezian analogy of intrinsic attribution of being, as this last obtains, say, between God and creatures or between a substance and its accident. Instead, between beings of reason and real beings, Suárez will allow only an extrinsic analogy of proportionality (I, 9).[32]

Another name for an extrinsic analogy of proportionality is *metaphor*.[33] Better said, such analogy occurs when a word is employed metaphorically. This has particular relevance in the present context of beings of reason. When the word "being" is used of an item such as a chimera or a goat-stag it is used metaphorically. When Suárez then says that beings of reason [focusing on them inasmuch as they terminate concepts and have (or are) merely objective being] have only a name in common with real being, he is saying that at most between beings of reason and real beings there is an analogy of the sort that obtains between "a smiling meadow" and "a smiling man."[34] Such an analogy involves more than mere homonymy. It is not complete equivocity (e.g., as in "trunk" as said with respect to elephants and trees).[35] However, it is at best the transfer of a word and a connection of the first and second instance of its use on nothing more than an extrinsic basis. That is to say, there is nothing in the meadow which justifies the transfer of the word "smiling" to it. The reason for the transfer is not in it but in us, in our perception and in our comparative judgment.

Similarly here, between real (whether actual or possible) being and purely intentional (in the crux case, *impossible*) being, there is no intrinsic community. For a purely intentional being, especially of the sort that is ultimately under discussion (e.g., a goat-stag or a square circle[36]), is one

---

32. On the Suarezian analogy doctrine, cf. esp. my article: "Suárez on the Analogy of Being," *The Modern Schoolman*, XLVI (1969), pp. 219-249, 323-341.
33. On this, see, e.g., *DM* 8, 7, nn. 21-22 (XXV, 302-303); *DM* 28, 3, n. 4 (XXVI, 13-14); *ibid.* n. 11 (16); *DM* 32, 2, n. 13 (323); *DM* 39, 3, n. 1 (523); *ibid.* n. 12 (527); also, cf. note 51 below.
34. For Suárez using this analogy, cf., e.g., *DM* 8, 7, nn. 21-22 (XXV, 302).
35. For one of Suárez's disciples affirming a pure equivocity between real being and being of reason, cf. P. Hurtado de Mendoza, S.J., *Disputationes metaphysicae*, d. 19, sect. 4, n. 77 (ed. Lugduni, 1624), p. 924.
36. In his article, "El Ente de razón en Suarez," *Pensamiento* IV, número extraordinario (1948), pp. 271-303, Juan F. Yela-Utrilla (p. 294) gives this example without text. I have not found it in Suárez, but I agree that it would be acceptable to him. For the square circle in the Jesuit tradition after Suárez, cf. Maximus Mangold, S.J., *Philosophia recentior*, Tomus prior (Ingolstadii, 1765) *Ontologia*, d. I, a. 1, n. 3 (p. 51).

which simply cannot be. Therefore, it is not being. Rather, it is "non-being" or nothing. Hence, any use of a common term between it and real being will have to be extrinsically justified. It will have to be a matter of metaphor.

This begins with the term "being." But by immediate inference it includes the terms "one," "true," and "good," the so-called transcendentals. It also includes more restricted terms one might employ to speak of such purely intentional "beings" as chimerae and goat-stags. For example, if one were to fabricate the impossible reality of a goat-stag running at a certain speed, in a certain time, and in a certain place, all of the terms that would be used to describe it would be transferred from their original proper settings, where they would designate real properties and attributes, and would be applied (like "smiling" to a meadow) in some other "not proper" setting on some entirely extrinsic basis or with some entirely extrinsic warrant.[37]

It may be recalled here that beings of reason are not intrinsically intelligible. Known only through other things in whose manner they are fashioned, beings of reason appear at best to be intelligible in a merely extrinsic way. While Suárez has nowhere to my knowledge expressly distinguished between intrinsic and extrinsic intelligibility, the distinction is implicit in what he has said. Made explicit among 17th century Scholastic doctors, it will provide an objective basis for truth and meaning with regard to even impossible beings of reason. Morover, it will give rise among those doctors to a major, but to this date largely unexplored, concern for "super-transcendence."[38] In this concern, Suárez's successors may have anticipated Kant's recognition of the supreme concept of the object in general (*der Gegenstand überhaupt*) which is presupposed by the division into possible and impossible.[39]

---

37. For a hint of this, see "... fictitious things, or beings of reason, are not said truly and properly to endure, because they do not exist. But in the way in which they are fabricated, or apprehended as if they existed, they are also conceived as if they endured, and this belongs or is attributed to them insofar as the act of the mind by which they are fashioned or for which they are objects, endures and exists." ("... res autem fictae, aut entia rationis, vere ac proprie non dicuntur durare, quia non existunt; sed eo modo quo finguntur, vel apprehenduntur ac si vere existerent, concipiuntur etiam ac si durarent, et hoc ipsum convenit vel attribuitur eis quatenus durat et existit actus mentis, quo finguntur, vel cui objiciuntur.") *DM* 50, s. 1, n. 1 (XXVI, p. 913). Among 17th century Jesuits following Suárez, Thomas Compton Carleton (*Philosophia universa. Logica*, d. XVII, s. 1, nn. 1-2 [Antwerpiae, 1649], p. 79) makes the point that a being of reason can be imagined to be in place and therefore to have local motion (on whose succession time could be founded).
38. This is the area which I have begun to survey in my article, "'Extrinsic Cognoscibility' ...," mentioned in note 1, above.
39. For this, see I. Kant, *Kritik der reinen Vernunft*, A 290; and *Metaphysik der Sitten, Einleitung*, III (AK VI, 218n). For just one of Suárez's successors here, cf. Maximilian Wietrowski, S.J. (1660-1737), *Philosophia disputata, in qua comprehenduntur con-*

Backing up a bit in *Section I*, we can see Suárez's initial consideration of causes and occasions for beings of reason (I, 8). There is first, he tells us, the intellect's pursuit of such non-items as *negations* and *privations*, which can be conceived only in a fabricated likeness of being. Second, there is the imperfection of the intellect which, limited in its ability to conceive things in themselves, must be content with knowing them piecemeal by comparison with other things. This necessarily requires fashioning *relations of reason*. Third is the creative capacity (what Suárez calls the "fecundity" [*ibid.*]) of the intellect itself which is able to fabricate mental figments from true and real beings by uniting parts which cannot be combined in reality.

## D. Section II:

In *Section II* Suárez denies Aristotelian formal, material and final causes for beings of reason. In and of themselves, beings of reason have no final cause since they are not directly intended by nature or any agent. Any final cause which a man may have in confecting them is his not theirs (II, 1). While Suárez does not explicitly say so, the common Scholastic[40] distinction between the *finis operis* (i.e., the goal of the work) and the *finis operantis* (the goal of the worker) can bring out his meaning here. For a being of reason, a *finis operantis* may be present without implying or demanding the presence of a *finis operis*.

Likewise, in themselves beings of reason have no formal cause beyond the fact that they imitate a certain form. And because as such they do not inhere in any subject they have no material cause. However, just as being of reason in general has a "quasi-transcendence" so a particular being of reason may have a "quasi-material cause" and what amounts to (although Suárez does not use the expression) a "quasi-formal" cause as well.[41] For example, he says, when one refers to the circumscribed *species* "*man*," one is pointing to a "certain being of reason whose matter [i.e., content] is man but whose form is the relation of species" (II, 1).

---

*clusiones ex universa philosophia Aristotelis* (Pragae, 1697), P. I, *Logica*, concl. 13, cap. 1, n. 1 (p. 232) and *ibid.*, cap. 2, n. 4, as cited in notes 117 and 118 of "'Extrinsic Cognoscibility'...."

40. Cf., e.g., Carolus Boyer, S.J., *Cursus Philosophiae*, ed. altera (Buenos Aires, 1939), I, p. 356.

41. Cf. note 26, above.

Suárez's immediate concern, however, is not with final, formal or material causes of beings of reason. Rather, it is with their efficient cause, which is the human intellect. Yet this too is not a direct or immediate cause of beings of reason. It is, again without his actually saying it, a kind of "quasi-efficient cause." His reasoning is that a true efficient cause would be a cause of existence. But a being of reason does not exist in its own right. Instead its "existence" is its being thought. In line with this, the intellect efficiently causes a being of reason when it causes the thought whose object that being of reason is. That is to say, in Suárez's language,[42] what the intellect immediately causes is the *formal* concept, which is a real being in the category of quality. The action of the intellect stops here. But "the formal concept itself," he tells us, "terminates in some way, as at an *object*, at the very being of reason which is thought or fashioned" (II, 3). This then amounts to the intellect's being a kind of "quasi-efficient" cause of a being of reason. In Suárez's words: the action of the intellect "is called the effecting of that being of reason itself in a broad way and according to the limit of the subject matter" (II, 4).

This will prompt further questions (II, 5). Just what is the action of the intellect through whose efficacy a being of reason is said to result? Is it indifferently conception, judgment, or reasoning? Or is it one of these exclusively? Again, is it only the intellect which can effect beings of reason? Specifically, can the will or the imagination effect them as well? Finally here, is it only the human intellect which causes beings of reason? What of God's intellect or the intellect of an angel?

Here also (II, 6) Suárez deals with the connection between beings of reason and "extrinsic denomination." Occasion for this is furnished by an opinion attributed to the 14th century philosopher-theologian, Durandus de Saint Pourçain, who is said to have identified these two. In this opinion, such items as "to be known," "to be a universal," "to be a subject," or "to be an antecedent" are matters of extrinsic denomination. That is to say, they are terms used to label things from outside their intrinsic reality. But they are apparently also beings of reason. Accordingly, the opinion attributed to Durandus regards these two as identical.

Such identification leads to a number of "corollaries" (II, 7-9). Thus, if we by our acts of intellect produce beings of reason, would not the same be true of God? Would not God then, inasmuch as he would know creatures from all eternity, confer on them some kind of eternal being in his mind? Is this what Duns Scotus was after with his doctrine of

---

42. For this, cf. esp. *DM* 2, sect. 1, n. 1 (XXV, 64-65).

"diminished being" (*ens diminutum*)?[43] Again, it would seem that beings of reason would result not only through the intellect but through the will as well. For would not such items as "being willed" and "being loved" have a status comparable to "being known"? Indeed, paradoxically it might appear that beings of reason would arise without any dependence on vital activities. The reason is that, prior to any such activities of ours, extrinsic denominations exist in things themselves.

This last gives a clue to Suárez's opposition to the identification attributed to Durandus. As the *Doctor eximius* sees it, at least some extrinsic denominations in things are completely independent of our understanding.[44] For example, a column is in fact "right" or "left" of an animal independently of our noticing that fact. Thus denominations of this sort will be "within the ambit of real being" (*sub latitudine entis realis* [II, 14]).[45] As such, in contrast to beings of reason, they will fall under the object of metaphysics. Among the disciples of Suárez, especially Pedro Hurtado de Mendoza, S.J. (1578-1651) will develop this point of the reality of extrinsic denomination.[46]

By contrast, it should be noted that we may confer too much reality upon an extrinsic denomination and thus fabricate a being of reason. For example, we might regard "the being seen" which results from an act of sight as some "quasi-passion" (cf. IV, 1) of a wall which is seen (II, 16). Also note that we could have an extrinsic denomination resulting from a being of reason, which denomination would itself be a being of reason. For instance, in a later passage (VI, 3) he will tell us that in an imaginary succession one thing could be conceived to be prior or posterior to another. Such priority and posteriority would be extrinsic denominations which, as they would follow upon a being of reason, would themselves be further beings of reason. A comparable example might occur when one chimera would be imagined to be at the right or left of another. In this way, we could have a second, third, fourth (to infinity) level of extrinsic

---

43. On "diminished being", see Armand A. Maurer, "Ens diminutum: A Note on its Origin and Meaning," *Mediaeval Studies*, XII (1950), 216-222. Also cf. Etienne Gilson, *Jean Duns Scot: Introduction à ses positions fondamentales* (Paris, 1952), pp. 292-6.
44. For a contrary opinion, cf. Gabriel Vázquez, S.J. (1549-1604), *Commentariorum ac disputationum in primam partem Sancti Thomae*, disp. 115, cap. 2, n. 2 (ed. Lugduni, 1631), Tom. II, p. 32.
45. On this, see my article: "Prolegomena to a Study of Extrinsic Denomination in the Work of Francis Suarez, S.J." *Vivarium*, XXII, 2 (1984), 121-160, esp. 133-4.
46. For this, cf. Pedro Hurtado de Mendoza, S.J., *Disputationes metaphysicae*, disp. XIX, esp. sections 1 and 2 (Lugduni, 1624), pp. 942-952.

denomination based upon beings of reason, which denominations would not be "within the ambit of real being" (II, 14).

To the question of how many faculties can cause beings of reason, Suárez answers *only the intellect*. More exactly, the intellect causes such beings of reason not by its direct acts but in various ways by reflex or comparative acts (II, 16). He denies that any sense power causes beings of reason. For no sense power is reflective in the way required (II, 17). Equally, the will or the appetite exercises no such causality (*ibid.*). The human will may tend toward what in reality is not good as though it were a good. But in so tending it is not fabricating a being of reason, for the will supposes its object as represented by the intellect. Again, even though the will could in its own order be in some way reflective, e.g., it might love love, still in this it would not be fashioning any being of reason. Rather, it would be tending toward something that is real in itself or something which is proposed by the intellect. Likewise, when the will tends to some object because of extrinsic denominations or relations of reason it is not fashioning a being of reason. Instead, yet again, it depends in this upon the intellect.

From this general rule, he tells us (II, 18), the imagination may be excepted. For the imagination does sometimes fashion beings which in fact never exist, or even cannot exist. Examples are golden mountains, which are possible even if they never do exist, and chimerae which not only do not exist but also cannot exist.[47] The imagination can do this by combining appearances that in fact are not or cannot be combined in reality, which amounts to producing beings of reason. In such production, however, the imagination shares somehow in reason or understanding.[48]

Notably in this section (II, 19-24), Suárez has discussed the subtle but important question, already touched upon above in connection with Duns Scotus (II, 7): whether God forms or even knows beings of reason? The issue was much debated in the 16th and 17th centuries. Briefly, Suárez's position was that since beings of reason involve a certain fabrication, if

---

47. There is in this context a question about the ultimate status of a golden mountain. Strictly speaking, for Suárez, it is not a pure being of reason. Rather, it should be real and mind-independent (to the degree that any possible is such). For a view in some ways similar to that of Suárez, cf. A. Meinong, *On the Theory of Objects*, tr. Levi, Terrell, and Chisholm (N.Y., 1960), p. 82, where the possible golden mountain is contrasted with the impossible round square.
48. For a different view among Suárez's Jesuit contemporaries and successors, cf., e.g., A. Rubio, S.J., *Logica mexicana, Tractatus de ente rationis*, dub. 4, pp. 74-75; P. Hurtado de Mendoza, S.J., *Disput. metaphys.* d. 19, s. 5, n. 84, p. 955; and G. De Rhodes, S.J., *Philosophia peripatetica*, II, d. 2, q. 1, s. 2, n. 2 (Lugduni, 1671), p. 19.

not a falsity (III, 4), it would contradict the perfection of God to form them. However, because God knows everything that is in the power of his creatures, he can and does know beings of reason inasmuch as they may be formed by us. On this question, Suárez differed from his Jesuit order-brother, Gabriel Vázquez (1549-1604), who held that God not only does not form beings of reason but he does not even know them precisely as they are formed by us. For Vázquez, God knows, say, the positive elements making up a goat-stag (i.e., a goat and a stag) but he cannot follow us to put the two together in an impossible synthesis.[49] The rift here between the two great Jesuits was continued and enlarged by their Order-brothers in the decades which followed.[50]

## E. Section III:

*Section III* begins to explore what was by Suárez's time the traditional division of beings of reason into negations, privations, and relations of reason. The division itself, whose origin Suárez traces (III, 1) to Aristotle, comes under fire from two directions. Some would say it does not contain members enough to include all beings of reason. Against this, others would say it has too many members.

Proponents of this second position might argue that negations and privations are not produced by the mind but are real in things themselves. For instance, such items as blindness and darkness seem to be matters of fact. Again, they might argue, it is difficult to distinguish negation and privation each from the other. For both *per se* involve a lack of being or a fabrication of being. One might distinguish them inasmuch as negation does not relate to or connote a subject whereas privation does. However, this divides them not as beings of reason, "but as it were extrinsically in

---

49. For Vázquez's opinion, cf. esp. *Commentariorum ac disputationum in primam partem Summae Theologiae Sancti Thomae Aquinatis*, Tomus II (Venetiis, 1608), In Qu. 28, art. 2, disp. 118 (pp. 52-56). On the rivalry and doctrinal differences between Suárez and Vázquez, cf. R. De Scorraille, *François Suarez* . . . . , I, 283-314; II, 479-482.
50. For examples, cf. Antonio Rubio, S.J., *Logica Mexicana, Tractatus de natura entis rationis*, dub. 4 (pp. 76-78); P. Hurtado de Mendoza, S.J., *Disputationes metaphysicae*, disp. 19, sect. 6 (pp. 955-957); Diego Alarcon, S.J., *Prima pars Theologiae Scholasticae* (Lugduni, 1633), Tr. II, disp. 3, cap. 6 (p. 124 ff.); R. de Arriaga, S.J., *Cursus philosophicus* (Paris, 1637), *Metaphysica*, disp. 6, qu. 4, nn. 38 ff. (pp. 788-789); Francisco de Oviedo, S.J., *Integer Cursus philosophicus* (Lugduni, 1640), *Metaphysica*, cont. XII, punctum 7 (pp. 443-445); T. Compton Carleton, S.J., *Philosophia universa* (Antwerpiae, 1649), Logica, disp. 13, sect. 6 (pp. 79-80); Richard Lynch, S.J., *Universa Philosophia Scholastica* (Lugduni, 1654), *Metaphy.* IV, tr. 1, cc. 4-5 (III, 234-237).

real entity or in relation to real being" (III, 2). Finally, proponents of this second position could argue, both negation and privation must be conceived in relation to something else whose negation or privation they are. Thus, they cannot be justifiably distinguished from a relation of reason.

Suárez's immediate concern in this *Section* is to show that negations, privations and relations of reason are all indeed beings of reason, and that they are properly distinct from one another. To the assertion that they exist in fact and are therefore not distinct from real beings, his reply first concerns relations of reason and then negations plus privations.

Returning to a point he has made in *Section* I, and earlier in *Disputation* 47 of the *Disputationes metaphysicae*, Suárez denies any basic sameness between real and rational relations (III, 3). When the proponents of such sameness present their view, they assert that the two kinds of relation are indistinguishable in that precise character of "being toward another" which is constitutive of relation. In this way, they further assert a relation of reason is basically identical with a real relation. To this Suárez replies (*ibid.*) that in a rational relation the character of "being toward another" is not real but merely thought or conceived. Therefore, such relations, in what precisely constitutes them as relations, are fundamentally different from those which are real.

Further, he declares (*ibid.*), negations and privations of themselves do not entail any reality. Instead, they simply remove something real. In so doing they show themselves to be non-being rather than being. Hence, considered exactly, both negations and privations are neither real beings nor beings of reason. Also just as such, they are not fabricated. Rather, they belong to things themselves, although not in any positive way.

*The turning point* is reached, however, when negations and privations are conceived not only negatively but in the manner of some positive being. It is in this precisely that they take on the character of beings of reason. That is to say, a being of reason is fashioned when something which in reality is only a removal or a lack of being is conceived like something which exists in itself or in some subject. This, he tells us, is indeed an extrinsic (*extraneus*) and metaphorical (*improprius*)[51] way of

---

51. For places where Suárez has explicitly mentioned the extrinsic and improper character of metaphor, cf. *DM* 8, s. 7, nn. 21 and 22 (XXV, pp. 302-03); *ibid.*, 28, s. 3, n. 11 (XXV, p. 16); *ibid.*, 32, 2, n. 13 (p. 323); *ibid.*, 39, 3, n. 1 (523). In the tradition before Suárez, for St. Augustine referring to metaphor as the transfer of a word from its proper use to one which is improper, see *Contra mendacium*, c. 10; versión del P. Ramiro Flórez, O.S.A., in *Obras de San Agustín*, Tomo XII (Madrid: Biblioteca de Autores Cristianos, 1954). For places where St. Thomas has contrasted "metaphorical" with "proper," cf. *De fallaciis*, c. 4; *In Sent.* I, d. 45, q. 1, a. 4 c.; *In Sent.* II, d. 13, q. 1, a. 2 c; *Summa Theologiae* I, q. 13, a.3, ad 1.

thinking and speaking – but it is not false (III, 4). This last seems so for the reason that in such thinking or speaking we would not be asserting that such negations or privations actually exist in the way we are conceiving them.[52]

As for distinctions among the three members, Suárez first looks (III, 5) to the border between a relation of reason and the other two members. The foundation for our conceiving a relation of reason is never in a negation or removal of some entity but always in some positive reality which we cannot conceive perfectly except in the manner of a relation. Hence, we fashion relations of reason not in order to conceive in a positive way a negation or a lack of relation itself, but rather to conceive something else which is really positive and absolute in the manner of something relative.

This seems especially the case when the relation in question has at least some remote foundation in things themselves. For when it is founded only on our way of conceiving, it may at times be used to express some negation on the side of reality. This may be seen from the rational relation of *identity* of one thing with itself (which is to say that one thing is not different from itself).[53] But this is accidental to the task of a relation of reason. Negation and privation, however, generally designate in the manner of something absolute and positive according to reason even though by such designation we may be expressing only some lack (III, 6). For example, when we speak of "nothing," "absence," "evil," "death," "blindness," "silence," etc., we generally speak as though we were designating positive things.[54] But in truth we are not.

This distinction between negation and privation on one side and relation on the other is unaffected by our need to know and define a privation in relation to some positive thing. For this results from the fact that a privation is a particular lack which really exists in something. It does not come from conceiving a being of reason in the manner of something positive. Moreover, the relation involved here is not "a relation according to being" but rather "a relation according to being said" (III, 7). That is to say, a privation is not as such really related to a positive thing whose privation it is. Rather, a privation is such that it cannot be thought of or

---

52. On the doctrine of "non-ultimate" conception which is involved in this, cf. my article, "Suárez on Beings of Reason . . . ," esp. notes 22, 23, 130, 131, and 138.
53. On this, cf. *DM* 7, s. 3, nn. 2-5 (XXV, 272-3).
54. It is worth noting that things of this sort are of central concern for modern existentialist thinkers such as Heidegger or Sartre, cf. J. Roig Gironella, S.J., "Investigación sobre los problemas que plantean a la filosofía moderna el ente de razón," *Pensamiento*, 11 (1955), 285-302, esp. 285-287.

spoken about except as the privation of something. In this way there can be a privation of a real relation which is not conceived as a relation even though it cannot be known or spoken of without a terminus. An example would be "to be an orphan," which would immediately imply the lack of the relationship of sonship. But while being an orphan cannot be understood without understanding a relation to a parent, it is, nevertheless, not itself conceived in the manner of a relation. Instead, we conceive and speak of it as a certain condition or absolute disposition which remains in the son when the parent dies (*ibid.*). Suárez's point then is that, even when a privation is the absence of a relation, we do not think of it as a relation, but rather as something absolute. Hence, even in this case there is daylight between that being of reason which is a privation and that which is a relation.

Finally in this *Section*, Suárez tells us (III, 8) privation and negation are no doubt distinct from each other. While privation expresses a lack in a subject which is naturally disposed to have what it lacks, negation expresses a lack absolutely and without qualification. In this connection, negation may be understood in two ways. First, in general, it may encompass both negation and privation which may thus together be divided from a relation of reason. Then, more particularly, negation may be divided from privation inasmuch as negation expresses a lack in a naturally non-suitable subject while privation expresses a lack in a naturally suitable subject. In this way, the original threefold division of beings of reason may be divided as positive (which is co-terminous with relations of reason) versus negative (which would be quasi-absolute). Again, negative would be divided into negations and privations (III, 9). To schematize this:

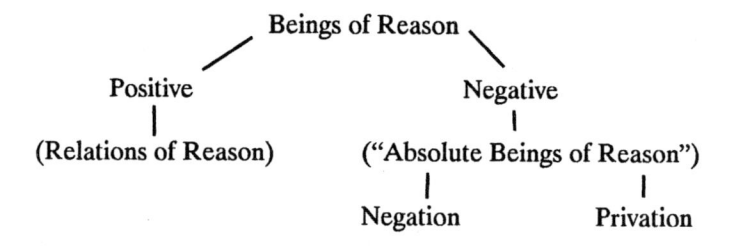

```
                    Beings of Reason
                   /                \
            Positive                  Negative
               |                         |
      (Relations of Reason)    ("Absolute Beings of Reason")
                                    |            |
                                 Negation    Privation
```

## F. Section IV:

The question remains as to whether the traditional division includes all beings of reason. One reason for doubting its sufficiency is that beings of reason do not seem restricted to negation, privation, and relation, but are apparently found throughout the Aristotelian categories (IV, 1). Thus in the category of *substance*, we can apparently conceive a chimera. In the category of *quantity* we can conceive imaginary space or we can conceive our chimera having certain quantitative features. Similarly, we can conceive beings of reason in the category of *quality*. We can imagine species of quality – habits or dispositions, powers, affections, and figures[55] – which are in fact beings of reason. For example, we can imagine fame and reputation to be dispositions, or jurisdiction to be a power (*ibid.*), i.e., qualities existing in subjects. Once more the chimera may be conceived as possessing qualitative features as well as quantitative ones. In much the same way it may be conceived to have other categorical features as well. Thus we can easily conceive a chimera to be *acting* or *undergoing* some action, to be in its own *place* or *time*, etc.[56] In yet another way, *action*, which to Suárez's mind is not some form inhering in an agent,[57] can be conceived so to inhere, which is to make it a being of reason (*ibid.*). Equally, such extrinsic denominations as "seen," "known," or "loved," may be conceived as categorical *passions* intrinsic to a thing which is denominated – and with that take on the status of beings of reason (*ibid.* and II, 16). Also in the category of *time*, we can in a Platonic way[58] fabricate an imaginary successive duration, outside of and prior to all moving things of our experience. Or we can conceive extrinsic denominations as though they were something in things which are temporally denominated. For example, from the motion of the sun we can designate events on earth as past, present, or future.[59] Accordingly, the argument concludes (*ibid.*), beings of reason cannot be restricted to just three members but must instead be divided through many more members.

Immediately in answer, Suárez tells us (IV, 2) that the traditional division can be taken in two ways. First, taken in a way which is not Suárez's preferred way, it may comprise only beings of reason which have some foundation in reality, but which would then receive their completion from reason. Examples include the character of being a universal, or being a genus. Negations and privations would also be of this kind. That is to say, although these are found really in things, they would become beings of reason precisely as they are conceived in some positive fashion by the intellect. By contrast, there are other beings of reason which are totally fabricated by the intellect, without any foundation in reality. An example

---

55. For Suárez on the species of quality, cf. *DM* 42, ss. 2-6 (XXVI, 607-632).
56. Cf. note 37, above.
57. Cf. *DM* 48, s. 4, n. 15 (XXVI, 892).
58. Cf. *Timaeus* 37B-38C.
59. Cf. *DM* 40, 9, n. 5 (XXVI, 585).

would be our, by now belabored, chimera. According then to this first way, what is divided by the traditional division is the being of reason which has a foundation in reality. On the other side, beings of reason which are mere fictions without foundation may range through all the categories or be framed in imitation of all the categories.[60]

But even if one were to follow this way, a question would remain as to why positive beings of reason with a foundation could not be multiplied through at least several categories (IV, 3). Why, that is, should every positive being of reason with a foundation be relative? Cannot many such beings of reason be thought of as qualities, actions, or passions?

A common answer in Suárez's time was derived from the proper mark of relation as such, i.e., "to be toward another" (IV, 4; cf. III, 3). For taken just as such, "to be toward as toward," does not entail anything inhering in a thing which is related. However, non-relative accidents do properly entail something inhering. Accordingly, a being of reason conceived as some positive accident must always be conceived as something relative. For only "being toward," inasmuch as it does not entail inherence, can be thought as attached or added on by reason. By contrast, non-relative accidents do entail inherence which, inasmuch as it always involves real existence, precludes their being mere creations of reason.

Suárez does not much like this answer, which is linked with a well known interpretation of St. Thomas's text (I, q. 28, art. 1). He himself thinks (IV, 5) that "to be toward another" does entail real inherence, or at least that "being toward" does not prescind from "being in."[61] But even so, he says, reason does fashion fictitious "being toward." *Ab aequo*, he sees no barrier to the same as regards inherence or "being in." Moreover, he contends, not all the categories of non-relative accidents entail true inherence. For some categories, such as *habitus*, the entailment is instead one of being extrinsically adjacent, contiguous, or juxtaposed. Hence, following the logic of this answer, such categories also would present a basis to be fashioned by reason. Finally, he rejects the interpretation of St. Thomas's text given by Cajetan and others to the effect that "being

---

60. For an opinion like this in the time immediately after Suárez, cf., e.g., A. Rubio, S.J., *Logica mexicana* (Lugduni, 1620), *Tractatus de natura entis rationis*, dub. 3 (pp. 71-72); P. Hurtado de Mendoza, S.J., *Disp. Metaph.* (Lugduni, 1624), d. 19, s. 4, n. 70 and s. 5, n. 87 (pp. 953, 955). John of St. Thomas, O.P. (*Cursus Phil.* Log. II, q. 2, a. 1 [ed. Reiser: Taurini, 1930], p. 287) attributes a similar opinion to Serna [*Commentaria in Logicam Aristotelis*, Hispali, 1624] and to Cabero [*Brevis Summularum recapitulatio*, Vallesoleti, 1623]. For a later division between beings of reason which are pure fabrications and those which have some basis, cf. I. Kant, *Kritik der reinen Vernunft*, A 670.

61. Cf., e.g., *DM* 10, 3, n. 14 (XXV, 351).

toward" abstracts from real being and being of reason, which is their basis for this answer (*ibid.*).

Suárez's own answer is subtle and must be understood against the nominalistic nuances of his doctrine of relation. As he judges the matter, a categorical relation, which is ultimately identical with its foundation,[62] does inhere in a subject but in addition it stands apart from other accidents inasmuch as it includes a disposition to or a connotation of a terminus.[63] Accordingly, the intellect can focus on this latter while leaving inherence out of explicit consideration. In this way, there is in relative things a "peculiar character" – not found in other categories – "on account of which positive beings of reason can be conceived in the manner of relations" (IV, 6). They can be *conceived*, that is, without any entailment of real inherence which would contradict their status as the unreal confections of the intellect. Contrariwise, in a non-relative accident, whether it be inhering or simply adjacent, there is no basis for thinking some positive being of reason analogous to it.

Returning to the instances alleged at the beginning of this *Section* (n. 1), Suárez denies that there are positive beings of reason in the categories of *quantity, time* (IV, 7), *quality* (IV, 8), *action*, and *passion* (IV, 9). With regard to imaginary space, rather than treating it as a quantity, he prefers to see it as a negation (IV, 7). Strictly speaking, there are no dimensions in merely imaginary space, which may be conceived as space not only where there are bodies now, but also to infinity beyond the last heavenly sphere.[64] Such imaginary space would be a pure void without any length, breadth, or depth. Of itself nothing, it would become "something" only when we conceive it and speak of it in a positive way (*ibid.*).

It would be rash to claim that Suárez here marks a decisive turn away from the main Greek estimate of "the void" ( τὸ κενόν ) as non-being[65] and therefore unintelligible.[66] Yet I do think that his thought is a departure from much that has gone before. For even though he would deny the void the status of a "*quantity*" of reason he would allow it to be a "*being*" of reason and to have in that a "secondary intelligibility."[67] Connected

---

62. Cf. *DM* 47, 2, nn. 12-22 (XXVI, 789-792).
63. On a longstanding controversy here among the disciples of Suárez, cf. my article, "Prolegomena to a Study of Extrinsic Denomination . . . ," n. 66.
64. Cf. *DM* 51, 1, n. 24 (XXVI, p. 979). On the relationship between such imaginary space and the divine immensity, cf. note 105 below.
65. This was true even for the Atomists; cf. Aristotle, *Metaphysics* I, c. 4, 985b 4-7.
66. See esp., notes 4 and 8, above.
67. For Suárez attributing a "secondary intelligibility" to beings of reason, see *De Anima* IV, cap. 1, n. 4 (III, p. 714).

with this: while for the Greeks (excepting the Atomists) and their successors the void could never be part of a scientific explanation, the way seems open now for what Suárez would call (IV, 2) a "doctrinal" use of the void.[68]

On the subject of *time*, in earlier *Disputations* Suárez had introduced a distinction between intrinsic and extrinsic time.[69] Intrinsic time is identical with the duration of things in motion. Accordingly, there are as many intrinsic times as there are things in motion.[70] Extrinsic time is present when the duration of one thing is measured by another. Again, the most obvious example is when the duration of sublunar things is measured by the motion and time of the heavens.[71] Intrinsic time, which is only rationally distinct from motion, is not a being of reason. As for extrinsic time, Suárez, following Aristotle,[72] regards measurement as a species of relation, and further thinks that reason and will are required in order to measure one duration by another.[73]

This leaves imaginary time, outside of and prior to all things in motion. Such would be impossible of realization and therefore it evidently would be a pure being of reason. But rather than being classified as something positive under the category of time, the figment of imaginary time, like that of imaginary space, would belong under negation (IV, 7). Strictly speaking, it is nothing; it becomes "something" only when we conceive and speak of it in a positive way.

As for the examples of honor and fame, Suárez denies (IV, 8) that these are "qualities of reason" (my quotation marks) and affirms instead that they are extrinsic denominations from real dispositions in those honoring or regarding. They are thus not beings of reason at all, but rather (however tenuously) real beings. For, as we have seen, extrinsic denomination (with exceptions such as those remarked in "D. *Section II*," above) falls under the ambit of real being. At the same time, if we somehow reify these denominations and think of them as qualities in the things denominated (i.e., in those honored or regarded), by that very fact we make them beings of reason. However, they do not in this become qualities of reason. Instead, they are conceived somehow as relating the

---

68. Cf. *Translation*, note 121 below.
69. Cf. *DM* 40, 9, n. 10 (XXVI, 586).
70. Cf. *DM* 50, 8, n. 6 (XXVI, 950); *ibid.* 10, n. 11 (961).
71. Cf. *DM* 5, 9, n. 9 (XXV, 198-199); *DM* 40, 9, n. 10 (XXVI, 586); *DM* 50, 10, n. 9 (XXVI, 960).
72. Cf. *Metaphysics* V, c. 15, 1020a 26ff; *Physics* IV, 223a 16-29.
73. Cf. *DM* 50, 10, nn. 8-12 (XXVI, 960-961). Also see notes 106 and 109 below.

things denominated to something else. That is to say, fame or honor would be nothing more than the one who is famous or honored being related to the recognition of others.

With regard to dominion or jurisdiction, Suárez tells us (*ibid.*) that this too is conceived in the manner of a relation. Thus, to have dominion is to be superior to someone. But being such is a relation of reason which is founded upon an extrinsic denomination from some will (which, of course, could be in turn based upon some physical power or condition). Thus, someone would have dominion, and someone else would be subject to that dominion, inasmuch as one would be established as superior and the other as inferior.[74]

Continuing to deny alleged non-relative categories of beings of reason, Suárez distinguishes *action* as twofold: immanent and transient.[75] Immanent *action*, which has no effect outside the agent, is not categorical action. It belongs in the first species of the category of quality,[76] and as such it will really inhere in an agent.[77] Accordingly, to conceive it so to inhere is not to fabricate a being of reason (IV, 9). By contrast, transient action, which has an effect outside the agent, is categorical action;[78] it does not inhere in the agent;[79] and to conceive it as so inhering would be to form a being of reason. However, such would not be an "*action* of reason." Instead, inasmuch as to inhere in an agent runs counter to the very nature of action, the only way it could be conceived as so inhering would be by changing its nature. It would have to be conceived not in the manner of an action but in that of a relation (*ibid.*).

As for the category of *passion*, inasmuch as this always entails inherence in a subject, to conceive it as such is not to conceive a being of reason. But what of conceiving denominations like "seen," "known," or "loved," as intrinsic to things which are so denominated? Would that not make them "*passions* of reason?" No, he says. For such would either still be extrinsic denominations, within the ambit of real being, or they would

---

74. For some treatment of Suárez on dominion and jurisdiction within civil society, cf. my article, "Francisco Suárez: On Preaching the Gospel to People like the American Indians," *Fordham International Law Journal*, 15, n. 4 (1992), pp. 879-951, esp. 890-896.
75. For the differences between these two, cf. *DM* 48, 2, n. 21 (XXVI, 879). On this subject, cf. J. Patout Burns, "Action in Suarez," *The New Scholasticism*, 38 (1964), pp. 453-472, esp. 462-466.
76. Cf. *DM* 42, 5, n. 15 (XXVI, 626).
77. Cf., e.g., Suárez, *De Angelis* VI, c. 6, n. 23 (II, p. 663).
78. Cf. *DM* 48, 2, n. 2 (XXVI, 874).
79. Cf. note 57, above.

be fabricated in the manner of relations of the thing denominated to some denominating act of seeing, knowing, or loving.

At this point, he is still within the first explanation of the division, an explanation which excludes totally fabricated items such as chimerae (IV, 2). Nevertheless, within this limited field, "it is clear that every denomination of reason which is produced in the manner of a positive form, and not in order to conceive or to declare some privation or negation, is produced in the manner of a relation" (IV, 9).

It is here (IV, 10) that Suárez introduces a second way to divide beings of reason sufficiently into negations, privations, and relations. While the first explanation of this division was clear and suitable enough, this second way has the important merit of being adequate for every being of reason, including chimerae and other impossible or "prohibited" items (I, 8). Such items, whether they be fabricated like substances or like accidents, are simply non-beings and thus, in this second explanation, are included under negation.

While in this particular place Suárez does not explicitly declare, "this second explanation is mine," it seems clear that it is his way of looking at the matter. It further seems clear to me that here we are reaching the core of Suárez's teaching on beings of reason. For without denying other such beings, it seems that impossible items more than any others are at the heart of his thinking. More than any other beings of reason, impossible things, inasmuch as they are self-contradictory (*repugnantia in se*),[80] are pure fabrications which have "being only objectively in the intellect" (I, 6). Accordingly, more than any other things, impossible items would appear to be necessarily included in any classification of beings of reason.[81]

This second explanation then recommends itself as Suárez's own inasmuch as it has room under negation for impossible items, such as a horse-lion, a flying ox, a goat-stag, or a chimera. In any event, with this explanation as well as with the first, "it is clearly evident that the division is sufficient, and the fact that beings of reason can be fashioned throughout all the categories does not contradict it. For, besides relations, all the rest are framed in the manner of privations or negations" (IV, 10).

---

80. Cf. *DM* 3, 2, n. 13 (XXV, 111). Also cf., e.g., ". . . for a chimera is an object including in itself two predicates which are repugnant to existence." (". . . chimaera enim est objectum in se includens duo praedicata, quae repugnant existere.") P. Hurtado de Mendoza, S.J., *Disputationes Metaphysicae* (Lugduni, 1617), disp. 2, sec. 1, n. 7 (p. 1035).

81. For a fuller treatment of what is involved here, cf. my article, "Suárez on Beings of Reason and Truth (1)," esp. pp. 69-75.

## G. Section V:

In *Section* V, Suárez extensively compares and contrasts negations and privations. Both truly belong to things themselves inasmuch as one thing really is the negation or the privation of another even apart from any consideration of ours (V, 2). As he already said (III, 4), at what was called "the turning point" of his doctrine, negations and privations become beings of reason only when we consider them in the manner of being (*ibid.*), i.e., only when we in our minds give them some fabricated positive reality.

As they are found outside the mind, in things themselves, negation and privation are similar in at least four ways. First, they both consist in a removal of some real thing or perfection (V, 3). Second, they are each respectively the extreme of a contradictory opposition which is found in reality and not just fabricated by the mind (*ibid.*). Third, both negation and privation have a basis in the very realities which they remove, albeit in different ways (V, 4) which we will consider below. Fourth, they agree in the fact that inasmuch as both belong to things themselves,[82] they can be predicated of those things without having recourse to any intellectual fabrication (V, 5).

This predication, which Suárez says (V, 6) is itself first "by way of division or negation" (*per modum divisionis seu negationis*), simply removes one thing from another. For example, "the man is not seeing." Predication of this sort expresses a negative judgment, which if true is itself the mental counterpart of either a total or a partial defect of being in things. In contrast to this, the predication of negations and privations can take place also "by way of composition and affirmation" (V, 6) (*per modum compositionis et affirmationis*). For example, "the man is blind" or "the man is non-seeing."

When we predicate negations or privations in this second way, we do somehow conceive them as being (cf. III, 4). For in this second way, through the positive copula, "is," being is somehow attributed to that which has no being. And in this attribution we have an inchoative basis for regarding negations and privations as beings of reason (V, 6).

Nevertheless, when we actually predicate negations and privations by way of affirmation, Suárez says (*ibid.*), we do not predicate the precise mode in which we conceive them. Instead, we leave this mode aside and predicate only what is conceived or ultimately signified, i.e., the lack of some reality (*ibid.*). Accordingly, when a negation or a privation is predicated in this second way, it is signified not as positing some being or reality in its subject, but rather as removing such.[83] In this manner, inasmuch as both remove rather than posit, the second way of composition becomes equivalent to the first way of division – and by the copula which the second way contains there is not affirmed any positive reality but "only the truth of cognition" (*ibid.*).[84]

To be sure, explicit beings of reason may be formed along with, or in the wake of, predications of negations and privations by way of affirmation. Thus, as was already said, negations and privations can become beings of reason precisely when we conceive them as positive independent realities (cf. III, 4).[85] They are in this way given a quasi-ontological density which they would not otherwise have. In accord with this, Suárez can at times say that privation as such is a being of reason.[86] But again, with total consistency, he can say that privations as such are not fictions; they are simply defects of being, i.e., in no manner themselves beings, either real or rational (cf. III, 3).

Between negations and privations, considered as they are in things, there are a number of differences. A negation does not need a real subject naturally apt to receive an opposite form, while a privation does require a subject of this sort (V, 7; cf. III, n. 8). Privations thus always inhere in something; but not so negations – for example, absolute nothing does not inhere in anything (V, n. 8). (For this reason, as we saw, an imagined absolute space or absolute time will be classed under negation rather than strict privation [cf. IV, 7].) In this way a pure negation differs not only from a privation but also from a partial negation, a not being this or that, which inheres in some positive thing or is conceived as so inhering (V, 25).

In the wake of this first difference between negations and privations as they are found in things, Suárez finds further distinctions among privations. Following Aristotle, he says privations as found in things may differ inasmuch as the aptitudes which they involve are taken properly or improperly (V, 8). Again, privations may differ inasmuch as they are

---

82. Cf. also *DM* 4, 1, n. 12 (XXV, p. 118).
83. Cf. *DM* 11, 3, n. 8 (XXV, p. 366); also see translation, *Section* 1, n. 4 and *Section* 3, n. 3.
84. For much of what is involved here, cf. my article, "Suarez on Beings of Reason and Truth (2)," esp. pp. 56-60, 63-71.
85. Much the same can be said of merely possible things. When we conceive them as somehow independently real in themselves, we create a fiction, an "actual possible," as it were; cf. *DM* 31, 2, n. 10 (XXVI, p. 232).
86. For this, see *DM* 47, 10, n. 5 (XXVI, p. 822).

ascribed to things because of a generic aptitude (e.g., "blindness" in a mole, because of the generic aptitude of animals to see) or they are ascribed because of a proper specific aptitude (e.g., blindness in a man).[87] Or privations may differ as proper or improper within the same species on account of different times involved in their corresponding aptitudes. For example, while a toothless man in the full flower of life might be said properly to be deprived of teeth, a toothless infant would be said to be so deprived only in an improper way.[88] Most properly, then, a privation is present when its corresponding aptitude is in the thing which is its subject according to species and with all necessary circumstances (cf. *ibid.*).

Again privations may differ as either total or partial (V, 9). Once more from Aristotle,[89] Suárez offers the example of a thing which is not visible. This could be totally invisible if it were deprived of all color. Or it could be partially invisible if its color were dull or faded. In this second instance, while one might speak of privation, obviously there would be no privation with respect to the color that still remained in the thing.

This last raises a question as to whether among privations there can be some that are more or less (V, 10). Suárez says if we are speaking of a total privation the answer is no. Like a negation, a total privation is either present or not, with nothing between. Among partial privations, however, there can be more or less (*ibid*). This will be possible by reason of the positive realities to which they are opposed. For if a reality admits of different degrees of intensity, a privation of more of such degrees will be greater and a privation of fewer will be less (*ibid.*). For examples, one can easily think of light or sound and more or less shadow or stillness.

A second difference between negations and privations as found in things is that when a negation has a subject of inherence (i.e., when the negation in question is not pure), it can have a necessary foundation in that subject (V, nn. 4, 11). For example, the negation of a natural faculty for neighing or a natural faculty for roaring in a man is such that it stems necessarily from the very nature of the man (V, 4). As opposed to this, a privation such as blindness in a man does not stem necessarily from the

---

87. For this example, cf. Aristotle, *Metaphysics* V, c. 22, 1022b 25-26.
88. On this score, Aristotle speaks of "blind but not according to every age" (τυφλὸς δ' οὐ κατὰ πᾶσαν ἡλικίαν), without giving any concrete example; cf. *Metaphysics* V, c. 22, 1022b 28-29. Averroes continues to speak of blindness but gives the example of a puppy (*catulus*) which is sightless but not blind; cf. *In Metaph.*, V, c. 22, t. 27 (ed. Venetiis: Apud Junctas, 1562), 134v.; St. Thomas has the same example, but embroiders on the theme to say that a dog (*canis*) up until it is nine days old is not said to be blind; cf. *In Metaph.* V, c. 22, l. 20; ed. Cathala, n. 1072.
89. Cf. *Metaphysics* V, c. 22, 1022b 34-35.

nature of the man which is its subject. Instead, beyond its subject a privation is contingently based upon some further aptitude which the subject has, but which may or may not be realized (*ibid*.). Immediately flowing from this is the fact that, while negations must be necessarily predicated of their subjects, privations must be said of their subjects in a contingent way (V, 11). Furthermore, inasmuch as negations necessarily stem from the nature of their subjects, they are in a sense indifferent to the existence of those subjects and can be said of them with necessity even when they do not exist (V, 16). Thus we can (and must) say that a possible man would not have the faculty of neighing (V, nn. 4, 16).

Negations and privations as they are found in things are distinct in yet a third way. Between a negation and its opposite there is excluded any middle term, but not so between a privation and the reality which is opposite to it (V, 12). Immediately he tells us: "this can be explained through two affirmations, in which predicates, either contradictorily or privatively opposed, are predicated of the same subject" (V, 13). In a case of contradictory opposition, such as that between a negation and its opposite, there is no medium between the two poles. It will be a simple case of being or not being. However, in a case of privative opposition there is a medium between the extremes.

The reason for this is that a privation is not simply a negation, but rather a negation where there is an aptitude in a subject. Therefore, from the lack of this aptitude, a subject can exist to which neither of the privative opposites belongs. For example, a stone is necessarily either seeing or non-seeing, but, lacking the aptitude to see, it neither sees nor is it blind. In the case of a man, however, who would be a proper subject having an aptitude for sight, there cannot be anything between seeing and being blind. For opposites in this case would be contradictorily opposed. From this Suárez infers what he calls "a proportional agreement" between a negation and a privation. Just as between something positive and its negation there is nothing in between with respect to any subject whatever, so also for a proportionate subject (e.g., man in the instance of *blindness*) there is nothing between something positive and its privation (*ibid*).

Here (V, 14) he raises an interesting objection with ramifications for questions of intelligibility and truth with regard to beings of reason, especially pure fictions or so-called "prohibited beings." It seems there is some doubt about the principle of excluded middle with regard to an impossible being of reason such as a chimera. Applied to propositions, this principle requires that between two contradictory affirmations there is no middle ground (V, 13). Applied to things, it entails: "It is necessary simply either to be or not to be" – that is, between the contradictory opposites, being and non-being, there is no middle; either one or the other is the case, with nothing in between.[90] But as regards a chimera, such does not seem to be the case. Take the contradictory opposites, "white" and "non-white." It would seem that anything would be either one or the other. But a chimera is neither white nor non-white. Hence, rather than one affirmative proposition (either "the chimera is white" or "the chimera is non-white") being true and the other being false (as the principle of excluded middle would have it) the fact is that both affirmations are false, for the reason that they concern a subject which "stands for" nothing (V, 14).[91]

Suárez's first reply is that a negation has no middle (between itself and its contradictory affirmation), if it is taken as a pure negation. If, however, there is something positive mixed with it, on that account it would not be pure and it could have a middle. But now if this proposition is false, "the chimera is non-seeing" (or "the chimera is non-white"), it is false not because it simply negates seeing but because, "by way of affirmation," through the copula it falsely attributes to the chimera some entity or being (*esse*).[92] Accordingly, he reasons, in order that

---

90. For this and for the order obtaining between the principle of non-contradiction and the principle of excluded middle, cf. *DM* 3, 3, n. 5 (XXV, p. 113); also see, *ibid.* 3, n. 8 (pp. 113-114).
91. In the background here is the common Scholastic axiom, "An affirmative proposition whose subject stands for no thing [i.e., a non-supposing subject] is false." On this axiom with application to a chimera, see William of Ockham, *Summa Logicae* II, c. 14, in *Opera* I, ed. Boehner, Gal, et Brown (St. Bonaventure, N.Y., 1974), p. 287 and *Expositio in lib. Periherm. Aristot.* I, prooem., n. 9 in *Opera* II (ed. Gambatese et Brown; St, Bonaventure, N.Y., 1978) pp. 366-367; John Buridan, *Tractatus de consequentiis*, I, c. 5 (ed. H. Hubien; Louvain, 1976), p. 25; John Major, *Introductorium in Aristotelicam dialecticem totamque logicem* II, tr. 1 (ed. Lugduni, 1520), f. 31r. For other places in which Suárez has mentioned the axiom, cf.: his *De Eucharistia* d. 50, 2, n. 2; XXII, p. 325; *De Scientia Dei* II, c. 5, n. 12; XI, p. 359; and *DM* 31, 12, n. 44; XXVI, p. 296. On the truth of a negative proposition with a non-supposing subject, see *Categories*, c. 10, 13b 27-35, where Aristotle says that if Socrates does not exist, then the proposition "Socrates is not sick" is true. The kinds of question involved in all of this seem close to modern questions about *Sinn und Bedeutung* with respect to items like Pegasus or a unicorn; for some of this, cf. Gottlob Frege, "Ueber Sinn und Bedeutung," *Zeitschrift für Philosophie und philosophische Kritik*, 100 (1892), pp. 25-50, tr. in H. Feigl and W. Sellars (eds.) *Readings in Philosophical Analysis* (New York, 1949), pp. 85-102; Bertrand Russell, "On Denoting," *Mind*, NS XIV (1905), pp. 479-493; Willard Van Orman Quine, "On What There Is," *Review of Metaphysics*, 2 (1948), 21-38, reprinted in W. V. Quine, *From a Logical Point of View*, 2nd ed. (Cambridge, MA, 1961), pp. 1-19; and Leonard Linsky, *Referring* (London, 1967).
92. On the positive character involved generally in predicating such "infinite" terms as "non-seeing," cf. Aristotle, *Anal. Prior.* I, c. 46; 51b 5ff. I see a problem here from Suárez's viewpoint. If "A chimera is non-seeing" is false when "non-seeing" is taken infinitely, why should not *a fortiori* every affirmative predication of a positive predicate of a non-existing subject be false? Why should not "A chimera is a fictitious monster" or even "A chimera is a chimera," be false? But Suárez says both of these are true propositions; cf. *DM* 31, 2, n. 11 (XXVI, p. 232); *ibid.*, 12, n. 45 (XXVI, p. 297); and *DM* 8, 8, n. 10 (XXV, p. 311).

contradictorily opposed predicates ("seeing" and "non-seeing," "white" and "non-white") be mutually exclusive without any medium between, it is necessary that, when they are enunciated "by way of affirmation," they also (like privatively opposed terms such as "seeing" and "blind" [cf. V, 13]) be taken with respect to a "proper" subject, which would be some existing thing (*ibid.*).

Suárez's second answer denies the basic assumption of the objection. For of these two propositions ("the chimera is white" and "the chimera is non-white"), that which involves the negative predicate ("non-white") is true, even though its subject does not exist. This is especially the case if, as "the logicians" say, that negation is taken "negatively" and not "infinitely" (*ibid.*).[93] That is to say, the negation is placed on the verb rather than the predicate – to make the opposition fall between "the chimera is white" (a false proposition) and "the chimera is not white" (a true one). Or, as Suárez puts it a bit later: "although in the order of the sentence the negation is placed after the copula, nevertheless in its power and sense it falls upon it" (V, 16). But then it is necessary that the opposition be purely negative, otherwise it will in part include some affirmation, as was correctly said in the first reply, which thus appears to be true when that negation is taken "infinitely" (*ibid.*) – that is when the negation is placed on the predicate rather than the verb.[94]

In line with this, negations can be presently attributed (even by way of affirmation) *with truth* to beings of reason in the very strictest sense. For example, it is true to say "a chimera is a non-being," precisely as Aristotle declares it true that non-being is non-being (V, 16).[95] But inasmuch as

---

93. On the distinction between negations here, cf. Aristotle, *Perihermeneias*, c. 2, 16a 30-32, c. 10, 20a 32ff.; *Anal. Prior.* I, c. 46, 51 b 6ff; and among the "logicians," cf. D. Soto, O.P., *Summulae summularum*, II, c. 1, n. 5 (2nd ed.: Salamanca, 1554), f. 16v.; P. Fonseca, S.J., *Institutionum dialecticarum libri octo*, VIII, c. 32, D (ed. J. Ferreira Gomes; Coimbra, 1964 [original: Coimbra, 1575]), II, p. 712; A. Rubio, S.J., *Logica mexicana, In de Interp.* I, c. 1, q. 5, pp. 477-478; Gaspar Cardillo Villalpendo, *Summa summularum*, II, pars 2, cap. 9 (Compluti, 1590), p. 14.

94. If anything, I think Suárez's reasoning here highlights the problem mentioned in note 92, above.

95. There are two ways, he tells us (V, 16), to explain this. First, although such propositions have the form of an affirmation, "in meaning and signification" they are equivalent to negations. Second, it may be said that the copula in such a proposition is not bound to any particular time, because as the subject is conceived to be a figment the (infinite) predicate is intrinsically proper to it, with the result that the proposition itself is not only true but also necessary. On the distinction in late Scholasticism between "meaning" and "signification," with further regard to supposition, cf. E. J. Ashworth, "Chimeras and Imaginary Objects: A Study in the Post-Medieval Theory of Signification," *Vivarium*, XV (1977), esp. pp. 59-60.

privations require a subject to which they just contingently or accidentally belong, they can with truth be attributed only to real, actually existing things; for example, actual blindness in a man requires an actually existing man (cf. V, 15). However, with truth and necessity privations can be possibly attributed to non-existing things. Thus, it is necessarily true that some possible man could be blind. But rather than a privation, says Suárez, what would be attributed here would be a positive and intrinsic *capacity for a privation* (*ibid.*).[96]

Privations and negations also differ, he tells us (V, 17, 18), inasmuch as privation, but not negation, is numbered (along with form and matter) among the principles of natural things. The main reason for this is that true change (as opposed to a creation [cf. V, 18] or an annihilation), presupposes a subject which has some aptitude to gain some further determination. Lack of such determination, therefore, is a lack which exists in an apt subject. That is to say, it is a privation rather than a simple negation. It follows that privation can be a principle in natural things, not as some positively influencing cause of their being, but as a *terminus a quo* for their substantial and accidental changes (cf. V, 17-18).

After consideration of a side issue about the possibility of a regress from privation to possession (V, 19), Suárez comes to compare negation and privation inasmuch as both are beings of reason. As such, they differ in that privations, even when they seem to be the absence of different categorical perfections, are fashioned in the mind only as quasi-qualities affecting a subject (V, 20-22). To show this he runs through privations conceived to be in opposition to each of the categories, i.e., substance, quantity, quality, relation, action, passion, time, place, position, and habit. Each of them, for different reasons and with different nuances, he regards as either not properly a privation (as in the case of habit) or as a quasi-quality. His conclusion then, with respect to privations as beings of reason, is: "it seems correctly said that true and proper privation is universally apprehended and thought in the manner of a quality" (*ibid.*, n. 22).

In contrast, negation is fashioned as a being of reason in the manner of quality and of other categories as well (V, 23). For while negation may be at times fashioned as a quality in some subject, beyond that, negation as such, unlike privation, does not require a subject. Because of this, negation can be fashioned in the manner of other categories besides quality. This last is important for understanding the basic Suarezian taxonomy of beings of reason. For, as we have seen, rather than excluding

---

96. Cf. Suárez, *De Scientia Dei* II, c. 2, n. 12 (XI, p. 300).

impossible items from the traditional division of such beings into negation, privation, and relation, Suárez places them under negation. The reason is obvious. Inasmuch as they involve self-contradiction, impossible items are simply nothing and thus belong under negation. The independence then of negation from a subject will allow quasi-substances, such as a chimera, or a quasi-place and/or quasi-quantity, such as imaginary space having dimensions, or a quasi-time, such as imaginary time outside every succession or change, all to be subsumed under it (*ibid.*). Again, negation's independence from a subject will allow a conception of pure nothing (V, 24), for example, in the phrase "creation from nothing."[97]

Resulting from their different relations to a subject, at times negation and privation (precisely taken as beings of reason) are formally or essentially diverse, while at other times they are only accidentally or materially distinct (V, 25). Thus, between a negation not in a subject and a privation there is an essential (or quasi-essential [cf. V, 11]) diversity, comparable to the diversity which obtains between a substance and an accident, which would exist on essentially different levels. But between a negation in a subject and a privation, there need be no essential diversity. Instead, there suffices one which exists by reason of the forms to which each is opposed. What comes to mind immediately is the difference between the negation of the faculty for neighing in a man versus the privation of sight which is blindness. Both would be comparable to accidents in that they would be thought to exist in a subject. But they would differ inasmuch as one would be thought to remove a supposed ability to neigh, while the other would be thought to remove the perfection of sight (cf. V, 4). In this way there is also distinction, in comparison to a single subject, among negations themselves, e.g., between the negations in a man of a supposed ability to neigh and of a supposed ability to roar (V, 4), and privations themselves, e.g., between a being of reason which is blindness and one which is deafness (V, 25).

If a privation and a negation are of some form in comparison to different subjects, they do not seem to differ essentially inasmuch as they are beings of reason. Rather, they differ only as relating to their different subjects (V, 26). The example Suárez uses is an absence of sight in a man versus an absence of sight in an angel. As beings of reason, both absences seem much the same insofar as both have being only in thought. Their difference is in the fact that one is thought to be in relation to a man while the other is thought to be in relation to an angel. Consequent upon this,

---

97. For a contrasting view, look at the texts from Bergson, cited above in note 27.

an absence of sight considered in relation to an angel, which has no capacity for sight, is classified as a negation, while an absence of sight considered in relation to a man is classed as a privation (*ibid.*). Following again from this may be the difference between such an absence being thought an evil or unnatural (for the man) or not (for the angel) (*ibid.*).

Finally in this Section, Suárez tells us he is talking only about simple negations. For complex negations (i.e., negative judgments), regarding different subjects, can have essential diversity inasmuch as the propositions which express them may be necessary or contingent. That is to say, some such propositions (e.g., "a man is not seeing") will be only contingently true, while others (e.g., "an angel is not seeing") will be necessarily true (V, 27).[98] And the diversity between what is necessary and what is contingent seems evidently essential.

## H. Section VI:

On the positive side of the general division of beings of reason, a relation of reason is described as one which the intellect fashions after the manner of a real relation (VI, 1). Like other beings of reason "which in some way contribute to the knowledge of real beings,"[99] a relation of reason should have, at least remotely, a basis in mind-independent reality (VI, 2). There is, however, a difference between a relation of reason and both a negation and a privation inasmuch as the basis of such a relation is something positive (cf. III, 5).

At the same time, as relations of reason mimic real categorical (rather than transcendental) relations, they are "adventitious," that is, not necessarily based in the nature of what they relate (cf. IV, 6). Again, while relations of reason may have a positive foundation in reality outside the mind, precisely as they are relations – mimicking categorical relations – some have no foundation while others have only a partial foundation, inasmuch as they have none or only some of the conditions (i.e., a real subject, a real term, and a real foundation [VI, 2]) required for a categorical relation (VI, 6).[100]

---

98. Note that the former exemplified judgment is immediately based upon the nature of the angel, whereas the latter requires some condition which is extrinsic to the nature of a man.
99. And which are therefore "doctrinal" in the sense mentioned in *Section IV*, n. 2; cf. also *Prologue*, n. 1 and *Section I*, n. 2.
100. Cf. *DM* 47, ss. 6, 7, and 8 (XXVI, pp. 808-818).

This is to use the term "foundation" in at least two, or possibly, three ways. All "doctrinal" beings of reason, including relations of reason, are founded in reality. But, additionally, relations of reason inasmuch as they mimic real relations, which need (1) real subjects, (2) real terms, and (3) real foundations (using the word in a sense restricted to relation), have beyond other beings of reason further foundation which they can either totally or partially lack inasmuch as they lack any or all of these three.

In line with this, relations of reason can be sub-divided in a number of ways. First they can be partitioned into those which, precisely as having none of the conditions needed for a real relation, do not have any real (*ex parte rei*) foundation and those which have only an insufficient foundation (VI, 3). In the prior member are contained all those relations which are fashioned between or among other beings of reason, especially those which are "merely fabricated" (*mere conficta*), e.g., the relation of similarity between two chimerae or of dissimilarity between a chimera and a goat-stag, etc. (*ibid.*).[101] Again in this member are relations between two or more privations, e.g., that one dark place is like another, that in imaginary space there is distance, or that in imaginary time there is priority and posteriority (*ibid.*).[102] These last relations, he tells us, have, at least remotely, more foundation in independent reality than, e.g., relations among chimerae (*ibid.*).[103] But once more in this member, there belong relations between or among real possible things, e.g., the relation of temporal priority of a (non-existing) Adam to the Antichrist. These relations also have a greater foundation in reality inasmuch as their termini are not altogether mind-dependent. But as these last are apprehended in reflex manner precisely as termini, they are mind-dependent (*ibid.*), and in this they too would offer no real foundation.

In the second member (i.e., with some insufficient foundation) again there is a sub-division, on the basis of the various lacks such relations of

---

101. Here, once again, the Suarezian taxonomy of beings of reason is not restricted to those which have a real foundation in things themselves outside the mind.

102. Note that priority and posteriority here can only be extrinsic denominations, which as they follow upon a being of reason, would themselves be further beings of reason. A comparable example might occur when one chimera would be imagined to be at the right or left of another. In this way, we could have a second, third, fourth (to infinity) level of extrinsic denomination based upon beings of reason, which denominations would not be "within the ambit of real being" (*sub latitudine entis realis*). For discussion of the more normally realistic character of extrinsic denomination for Suárez, cf. J. P. Doyle, "Prolegomena to a Study of Extrinsic Denomination in the Work of Francis Suarez," *Vivarium*, XXII (1984), pp. 119-160.

103. Connected with this is the distinction in foundation between a relation of reason and both a negation and a privation, cf. *Section* 3, n. 5.

reason have of the conditions required for a real relation (i.e., a real subject, term, and foundation [VI, 2]). Thus under this member can be located relations in which only one of the terms is existing, e.g., the priority in time of an existing Peter to a future Antichrist or the diversity of Peter from a chimera (or vice versa) (VI, 4).[104] or even the presence of God in imaginary space.[105] In this order there can be a further subdistinction, inasmuch as the relations in question can be founded on any member of the traditional Aristotelian triad: (a) unity, (b) action, or (c) measure (VI, 4).[106]

Second, under this member can be located relations among extremes which although they are real are not really distinct. Again there is a new subdistinction here of (a) a relation which is entirely rational (*rationis ratiocinantis*), as, e.g., the relation of identity (or of distinction) of a thing with itself, and (b) a relation (*rationis ratiocinatae*) which has some virtual foundation in reality, as, e.g., the relation of distinction among the divine attributes (VI, 5).[107] Third, under this member belong those relations which lack an actually existing intrinsic foundation in either one or both of the extremes (subject and term). The latter, for instance, would be in conventional signs (whether these be words or things), which in both

---

104. Also cf.: *DM Index locup.* V, c. 11 (XXV, xxii).
105. Cf. *DM* 30, 7, n. 17 (XXVI, p. 100); and Suárez, *De Eucharistia* d. 54, 1, n. 4 (XXII, p. 255). For an closer relating of divine immensity and imaginary space among Suárez' Jesuit successors, cf. G. De Rhodes, S.J., *Phil. perip.* L. II, disp. IV, q. 1, s. 2 *de Loco et Vacuo* (Lugduni, 1671), p.219. On this question in Suárez, cf. J. Hellin, S.J., "Sobre la immensidad de Dios en Suarez," *Estudios eclesiasticos*, 22 (1948), pp. 227-263, esp. 253-257.
106. Cf. Aristotle, *Metaphysics* V, c. 15, 1020a 26ff. Let us note here that relations based upon the last member of the triad, i.e., measure, seem always to be rational. Indeed, they seem to be a subdivision of the relation of signification involved between deliberate signs and what they signify (On this, cf. C. Scheibler, *Opus metaphysicum*. (Giessae Hessorum, 1617) I, c. 25, pp. 825-844, esp.: "Sub signo et signato comprehenduntur mensura et mensuratum." ("measure and measured are contained under sign and signified"), p.825). On both sides, for Suárez such is a rational relation founded upon an extrinsic denomination (cf. note 109 below). Again let us remark that (perhaps with the exception of those mentioned in note 102, above) for Suárez such denominations are within the ambit of real being. And as such, they offer a minimal real foundation for rational relations which, as they are purely mind-dependent, are outside the ambit of real being.
107. For more on a distinction of reason, cf. *DM* 3, 1, n. 6 (XXV, p. 104). It may be noted here that, although a distinction of reason may be itself purely mind-dependent, between it and the *distincta* there may fall a real distinction, such as also falls between any being of reason and any real beings. This raises the further point of what kind of distinction falls between two beings purely of reason. In at least one place, Suárez says that such would be "quasi-real"; cf. *DM* 7, 1, n. 7 (p. 252). But elsewhere he appears to think that such a distinction would be rational; cf., e.g., *DM* 5, 2, n. 11 (p. 151).

extremes are founded upon a merely extrinsic denomination (VI, 6).[108] The same, he says, is true of the relations of reason between master and slave, husband and wife, buyer and seller, etc., all of which are founded on extrinsic denominations from the wills of the parties involved (*ibid.*).[109] Again, in this order belong all non-mutual relations insofar as they are rational in one of their extremes, e.g., the relation of seen to one seeing, of seeable to sight, or of knowable to knowledge, or also the relations of God to existing creatures (VI, 7). Fourth, there is another kind of relation of reason with some remote basis in existing things and some proximate foundation in an extrinsic denomination. Of this kind are those relations

---

108. Let us remark again that for Suárez an extrinsic denomination, inasmuch as it is within the ambit of real being *sub latitudine entis realis*, provides a certain real foundation for relations of reason, which, as such, are outside the ambit of real being.

109. In this can be seen something of the wide swath which Suárez's being of reason doctrine cuts into the order of the practical. For a somewhat similar freely willed choice in the extrinsic (and "rational") character of discrete quantity, cf.: "... if you consider a group of three men, in no one of them is there the first, second, or third unity; for no rationale of such order can be assigned among them; therefore that order, if there is any, is only one of reason...." ("... si ternarium hominum secundum se consideres, in nullo eorum est prima unitas, secunda, aut tertia; nulla enim ratio talis ordinis potest inter eos assignari; ille ergo ordo si quis est, solum est rationis....") *DM* 41, 1, n. 2 (XXVI, p. 588); also cf. *ibid.* n. 17 (p. 592). For a like subjectivity in the measurement of continuous quantity, cf. "... in genuine continuous quantity measure as such is always a matter of human adaptation, for if things are considered in themselves, there is no greater reason that this thing measure that, than vice versa." ("... in propria quantitate continua mensuram ut mensuram semper esse per humanam accomodationem, quia nulla est major ratio quod haec res mensuret illam, quam e converso, si res ipsae secundum se spectentur.") *DM* 40, 3, n. 8 (p. 540); *ibid.* 4, 6, n. 4 (XXV, p. 136). On this last, let us remember Scheibler (cf. note 106 above) treating measurement as a subdivision of signification. On its face, this would seem to be related to questions regarding scientific constructs, which some in the tradition dependent upon Suárez would regard as *entia rationis*; cf., e.g., the Calvinists, R. Goclenius: "An epicycle in astronomy is a being of reason, that is, it is located in the heavens not by the design of nature, but by human choice, as a fictitious hypothesis ...." ("Epicyclus in Astronomia est ens rationis, id est in coelo locatus est non naturae consilio, sed hominum arbitrio, ut fictitia hypothesis ....") *Isagoge in ... Primam Philosophiam* (Francofurti, 1598), c. 1, n. 1 (p. 15), and C. Timpler: "Thus one kind of being of reason has a foundation in things themselves, as for example the spheres and imaginary circles in astronomy, but another kind does not, for examples, Cerberus, a chimera, etc." ("Deinde aliud [ens rationis] fundamentum habere in ipsis rebus, ut sunt orbes et circuli imaginarii in doctrina sphaerica: aliud vero non, ut sunt cerberus, chimera, etc.") *Metaphysicae Systema Methodicum* (Hanoviae, 1616), I, c. 3, prob. 11 (p. 36). In this connection, let us note that for Timpler a mathematical point is a being of reason; cf. *ibid.* V, c. 2, prob. 7 (p. 505). Suárez, in contrast, regards the points of the mathematicians as having real physical existence; cf. *DM* 50, 4, nn. 1-68 (XXVI, 551-571), esp. see nn. 29-32 (pp. 559-560). For Suárez on the real character of the objects of mathematical abstraction, cf., e.g., *DM* 10, 3, nn. 19-21 (XXV, pp. 352-353). I have not found any place where Suárez discusses the character of mathematical constructs such as epicycles. But what he has said about the subjective character of measurement itself does seem relevant.

of reason which are called "logical intentions": relations of genus, species, predicate, subject, and the like. In these relations, at times, although the extremes are real, there is not enough distinction between them, as between animal and rational compared as genus and difference. Or, the opposite, at times there is not enough unity in actual existence (*in re*) as in the case of a universal with respect to singular things (VI, 8).[110]

In instances of this fourth kind, the proximate foundation is in an extrinsic denomination resulting from an act of the intellect (VI, 8). Since such acts are threefold: conception, judgment, and reasoning, relations of this fourth kind are likewise threefold (VI, 9). From conception, there arise relations of genus, species, definition, definitum, etc.; from judgment, relations of predicate, subject, copula, and proposition; from reasoning, relations of antecedent, consequent, mean, extreme, etc. (*ibid.*). These relations are not gratuitously fashioned; they have bases in things existing independent of the mind, bases such as: (i) real similarity (*convenientia*), (ii) real identity or real union of one thing with another (the basis for the relation expressed by the copula), or (iii) a real emanation of one item from another, or real concomitance, etc. (on which inference, whether *a priori* or *a posteriori*, is founded) (*ibid.*).[111] Relations of this kind, founded so immediately upon denominations coming from acts of the intellect, are in a special way (*peculiariter*) called "second intentions" (VI, 10). The reason for this is (in part, at least) that they are objects of a second formal intending (*ibid.*). Of course, the mind can further reflect on these second intentions – in order to form succeeding (3rd, etc.) intentions (VI, 11);[112] and so on to infinity (*ibid.*).[113] But any foundation which

---

110. Cf. also *DM* 6, 6, n. 12 (XXV, p. 228).
111. On similarity or likeness (*similitudo*) as a foundation for the abstraction which results in the (universal) objective concept, cf. *DM* 35, 3, n. 40 (XXVI, p. 452); *DM* 38, 1, n. 3 (p. 492). Let us note that real likeness among things comes in grades; cf. *DM* 2, 2, n. 18 (XXV, p. 76); *DM* 6, 9, n. 19 (p. 242); *DM* 31, 13, nn. 19ff. (XXVI, pp. 304ff.); *DM* 36, 1, n. 3 (p. 479). For a denial of real "identity" among different things at the first level, confronting the first operation of the intellect, cf. *DM* 6, 2, n. 13 (XXV, p. 210); also cf. *DM* 7, 3, nn. 3-5 (pp. 272-273). At the second level, confronting the second operation of the intellect, what is real is unity – identity is a relation of reason founded on that; cf. *DM* 4, 1, n. 7 (XXV, p. 117). At the third level, the obvious understanding of "emanation" and "concomitance" would connect the first with *a priori* and the second with *a posteriori* reasoning. However, on occasion, Suárez will treat both emanation and concomitance on what appears to be a single *a priori* line; cf., e.g., *DM* 18, 3, nn. 2-10 (XXV, pp. 615-619).
112. Cf. *DM* 54, 2, n. 17 (XXVI, p. 1023).
113. Cf. *DM* 6, 9, n. 20 (XXV, p. 242). Also cf. *DM* 15, 11, n. 19 (XXV, p. 563); and *DM* 3, 2, n. 13 (XXV, p. 111) where he explicitly speaks of multiplying certain beings of reason to infinity and calls them "useless" (*inutiles*); as well as *DM* 2, 6, n. 5 (p. 100) where he notes the mind's horror of a process to infinity. In this connection, consider A. Rubio on the unscientific character of those beings of reason which he regards as altogether without foundation: "... those things about which science directly treats must be definite. But beings of reason which have no foundation can be multiplied to infinity.

these second intentions have in existing things must be understood of the first relations of such a succession (*ibid.*).

## I. Conclusion:

As was indicated earlier, Francisco Suárez had great influence on seventeenth century philosophy. When one thinks of that century as the birthtime of so much of modern thought and of Suárez as summarizing so much of medieval thought, his role as a bridge figure begins to come into focus. To be sure, it seems to me that it was mainly across the Suarezian bridge that medieval Aristotelianism came into modern consciousness. For this, none of his works of theoretical philosophy was more relevant than the famous *Disputationes metaphysicae*.[114] And within this, the 54th Disputation, inasmuch as it deals with the very margins of what can be, what can be known, and what can be spoken of, was extremely important.

My personal interest is in Suárez himself and his impact most especially on the Latin philosophy taught in 17th century Catholic and Protestant universities. I have indicated a little of this with various notes in the previous section on Suárez's *Life* and in this *Introduction*. Let me now further disclose that my particular interest in the 54th Disputation revolves about issues connected especially with Scholastic understandings of intentionality.

Scholastic intentionality theory relates to a myriad of later items. Without pursuing them at this point, I would list among these: Descartes' concern with the formal and objective reality of ideas, Leibniz's principle of sufficient reason, as well as his interest in the relation of logic and metaphysics, and Berkeley's "*esse est percipi*" doctrine (which raises questions discussed by Suárez's successors about the entry of the act of cognition itself into the make-up of a being of reason). Beyond that and far

---

Therefore no science can directly treat of them." (... ea de quibus scientia per se agit, determinata esse debent: sed Entia rationis, quae non habent fundamentum, possunt in infinitum multiplicari ab intellectu; ergo nulla scientia potest per se agere de illis.) *Logica Mexicana, De natura entis rationis*, dub. 6, p. 79. For Suárez' recognition of such an objection, cf. translation, Section 4, n. 2. Also note again the parallel between this and Meinong's "homeless objects," cf. note 24, above.

114. In this I entirely agree with John Deely when he writes: "... it was the teaching of Suárez in the *Disputationes Metaphysicae* that became the *philosophia recepta* so far as Latin Aristotelianism was to be imbibed into the newly forming national language traditions of modern philosophy, particularly in France, the Netherlands, and Germany," in *Tractatus de Signis: The Semiotic of John Poinsot*, p. 45, n. 2.

beyond my purpose or opportunity to develop it now, I see some of the themes and interests of Suárez's 54th Disputation present in Brentano's explicit embrace of Scholastic intentionality theory and the development of this in directions of phenomenology and existentialism by such persons as Meinong, Mally, Husserl, and Heidegger.

Meinong, in particular, is important both for his own *"Gegenstandstheorie,"* with its consideration of "impossible objects," and also as a catalyst for Bertrand Russell. It is no secret that Russell's "Theory of Descriptions," so influential for the evolution of 20th century analytic philosophy, was developed first in reply to Meinong. Not far from this, and influencing Russell and others in this century, is Frege's *"Sinn und Bedeutung"* doctrine (which in ways runs parallel to Suárez's concern about the signification and supposition of a being of reason). In turn, both Russell and Frege have influence on persons like Quine,[115] Linsky, and a host of others.

Along the way, various other figures and doctrines have at least logical connections with or parallels to the intentionality theory of late Scholasticism, centering as this does on the construction of so-called "beings of reason." I think first of Kant's "Copernican revolution," and much of its aftermath in later philosophy, which puts such emphasis on objectivity and the role of the constructive reason. As mentioned above, I believe the important link here lies in "supertranscendence."

I think further of contemporary questions about "scientific constructs," about "logical fictions," about "literary fictions," about "error and falsehood," about Bergsonian "pseudo-problems" of evil and nothingness, and about Popperian questions regarding objective knowledge and its "third world." And finally, I see this 54th Disputation connected in a basic way with sign-theory, or semiotics. Thinking specifically of the clear divide which Suárez has fixed between real being and being of reason, I believe his work addresses an important ongoing question about the possibility of a unified semiotics in face of a main division of signs into those which are natural (i.e., real or mind independent) versus those which are conventional (i.e., mind dependent).[116] Although Suárez's

---

115. Professor Quine graphically represented the core issue of beings of reason, and the problem with which we began this Introduction, when he wrote: "This is the old Platonic riddle of nonbeing. Nonbeing must in some sense be, otherwise what is it that there is not? This tangled doctrine might be nicknamed Plato's beard; historically it has proved tough, frequently dulling the edge of Occam's razor." "On What There Is," in *From a Logical Point of View*, pp. 1-2.
116. I have addressed this topic before, cf. "Suarez on Truth and Mind-Dependent Beings: Implications for a Unified Semiotic," in *Semiotics* 1983 (New York, 1987), pp. 121-133. While I am not sure now of all that I said in 1983, this article will introduce the reader to the main question here.

Disputation may dictate a negative answer, and in that be unsatisfying for some semioticians, even for these it has the merit of sharply defining the basic question itself.[117]

---

117. See Deely in the place cited above in note 113.

## III. Translation Notes

In my view, Suárez was a very able philosopher. His thoughts command attention. But his writing style, like that of most Latin Scholastics, is dull, matter of fact, and repetitious to a fault. His sentences frequently run on and his paragraphs often seem interminable. Nevertheless, I have tried to translate his text as faithfully as possible.

At times, I did break up his long sentences into shorter ones. Also at times I substituted active for passive voice and I occasionally changed his impersonal and/or periphrastic constructions to a more colloquial form. Although I was often tempted, I did not restructure any of his often too long paragraphs. Instead, in these I have followed his composition and structuring. My intention throughout was to be at once faithful but also reasonable.

As every translator of Latin knows, there are difficulties in rendering that language faithfully, clearly, and consistently into readable English. Perhaps the most obvious difficulty is presented by the absence of both a definite and an indefinite article in Latin. In many contexts this makes little or no difference. But there are occasions when one must choose whether to supply an article or not, or, presuming an affirmative choice, whether to use a definite or an indefinite article. At times, the translator can only hope that his decisions are correct.

Again as every translator of Latin knows, some words offer particular problems. The prize example is furnished by the term *"ratio."* In different contexts, it can be translated as *reason, reasoning, argument, rationale, account, ratio, nature, essence, aspect, facet, character, feature, characteristic*, etc. The goal desired is to render it correctly and consistently, all the while attending to contexts and nuances. Of course, the difficulty with *ratio* is compounded here by the very terminology of the subject matter, i.e., being of *reason (ens rationis)*.

Hoping to aid assessment of the translation, I have sometimes indicated the presence of *"ratio"* by putting it in parentheses following an English equivalent. I have done the same with other words. An example would be *"habitudo,"* which in different contexts can mean *relation, reference, respect, disposition, condition, habitude*, etc. Or for another example, there was *"fingere,"* which can mean *to feign, to fashion, to fabricate, to make up, to fictionalize*, etc.

With much the same goal of aiding assessment, I have often included the original Latin word or phrase after a translation, especially if that translation was a bit free. Again, in hope of helping comprehension, I have supplied words [in square brackets] which are not actually in Suárez's text, but which seem clearly enough to be called for from the context. This last is again related to the vagaries of Latin, which generally understands but does not express certain words (e.g., personal pronouns in the conjugation of verbs, or the antecedents of relative prounouns or adjectives). I have translated the headings which appear in bold faced type from Suárez's own text. I have also employed brackets and parentheses to supply full names and dates at Suárez's first mentions of earlier persons. Finally, in addition to my *Introduction to the 54th Disputation* – which is largely a paraphrase of the text, I have added some notes to the text itself with the aim of clarifying especially arcane and difficult passages.

For the Latin source for this translation, I used Charles Berton's edition of Suárez's *Disputationes Metaphysicae* from the *Opera Omnia* (Paris: Vivès, 1856-1866). As I went along, I checked Berton's reading against that of two earlier editions: Salamanca, 1597 and Mainz, 1605. At times, I corrected Berton from these editions. But on occasion, I preferred his reading to theirs.

# Disputation 54

## On Beings of Reason

### [Prologue]

1. *Why We Are Treating Here of Beings of Reason.* – Although in the first Disputation of this work[1] we did say that being of reason was not included under the proper and direct object of metaphysics and it was, therefore, excluded from this treatise even by the Philosopher [i.e., Aristotle] himself in Book 6 of his *Metaphysics*,[2] nevertheless, I believe that it belongs to the completion of this doctrine and to the metaphysician's task to rehearse what is common and general about beings of reason. For the cognition and knowledge of these is necessary for human instruction. Indeed, without them we can hardly speak either in metaphysics itself, or in [natural] philosophy, much less in logic, and (what is more) even in theology. Moreover, the task cannot in fact belong to anyone else but the metaphysician. For, first of all, since beings of reason are not true beings, but as it were "shadows" of being, they are not intelligible through themselves, but by some analogy and conjunction with true beings.[3] Therefore, they also are not through themselves [scientifically] knowable (*scibilia*),[4] nor is there a science which has been instituted directly and primarily in order to know them alone. Indeed, the fact that some attribute this task to dialectics is a dialectical error. For the purpose of that science is only to direct and to reduce to art human rational operations, which [rational

---

1. Cf. *DM* 1, sect. 1, nn. 4-6; XXV, 3-4.
2. Cf. 1027b34-1028a3.
3. At times, Suárez says beings of reason have a "secondary intelligibility": cf. *De Anima* IV, cap. 1, n. 4 (III, p. 714). Seventeenth-century, especially Jesuit, thinkers will distinguish here between "intrinsic" and "extrinsic" intelligibility. While lacking the former, beings of reason will be said to possess the latter in common with real beings. On this, see my article, "'Extrinsic Cognoscibility': A Seventeenth Century Supertranscendental Notion," *The Modern Schoolman*, LXVIII (1990), pp. 57-80.
4. On the Suarezian notion of the "scientifically knowable" (*scibile*), cf. my article, "Suárez on the Unity of a Scientific Habit," *The American Catholic Philosophical Quarterly*, LXV (1991), pp. 311-334, esp. 327-333.

operations] are not the beings of reason of which we are now treating, but rather real beings.[5] Therefore, no craftsman (*artifex*) or no science directly and primarily (*per se primo*) aims at the knowledge of beings of reason, but this must be treated insofar as it is joined with knowledge of some real being. Thus a natural philosopher treats of privation, which is joined with matter relative to form, and treats of a void by comparison to place, and the same is true with regard to other [beings of reason].

2. In this way, then, it is proper to metaphysics to treat about being of reason as such, and about its common character, properties and divisions. For these features (*rationes*) in their own manner are quasi-transcendental and cannot be understood except by comparision to true and real features of beings, either transcendental or so common that they are properly metaphysical. For what is fictitious (*fictum*) or apparent must be understood by comparison to that which truly is. Accordingly, although other disciplines (*facultates*), like physics or dialectics, sometimes touch upon some beings of reason which are linked with their objects, as we just showed with examples, nevertheless they cannot out of their own resources (*ex propriis*) explicate the quasi-essential features of these. Therefore, this belongs, as it were, obliquely and concomitantly to the metaphysician, as Alexander [of Aphrodisias (fl. 200 A.D.)],[6] St. Thomas [Aquinas (ca. 1225-1274)],[7] and others note at Book VI of the *Metaphysics*. In this way they also explain Aristotle, as we noted above.[8] Accordingly, Aristotle himself, in his *Metaphysics*, did not leave these things out altogether, as it clear from Book IV, chapters 1 and 2,[9] and Book VII [sic], the last chapter.[10] Hence, we must consider the matter in the present Disputation, in which we will first explain in some way the nature and causes of this being. Then, with an added division, we will indicate the various classes of these beings, especially touching all those items which seem relevant to this doctrine [i.e., metaphysics].

---

5. Contemporaneously and afterwards, there was debate about whether or not the object of logic is itself, as Suarez said, real being or whether it is being of reason. On this, cf. Wilhelm Risse, *Die Logik der Neuzeit* (Stuttgart-Bad Cannstatt, 1964), esp. I, c. 5, pp. 308-439.
6. Cf. Alexander of Aphrodisias, *In Aristotelis Metaphysica Commentaria*, ed. M. Hayduck, in *Commentaria in Aristotelem Graeca*, I (Berolini, 1891), p. 458.
7. See St. Thomas Aquinas, *In XII libros Metaphysicorum Aristotelis expositio*, VI, c. 3, lect. 4; ed. M.-R. Cathala, O.P. (Taurini, 1950), pp. 311-312, nn. 1241-1244.
8. See *DM* 1, s. 1, nn. 4-6 (XXV, pp. 3-4).
9. Cf. 1003b 8-11.
10. For this, cf. *Metaphysics* VI, c. 4; 1027b 18ff.

## Section I
## Whether a Being of Reason Exists, and What Essence It Could Have.

1. On this matter, there are a number of positions which are sharply opposed to one another, at least in words. For if their authors are more closely examined, perhaps they are arguing only about words.

### The First Opinion: Denying Beings of Reason.

2. Thus, certain people flat out deny that there are any beings of reason, [maintaining] instead that all that is said of these, can very well be understood of things themselves and can be preserved in these latter. [Francis of] Mayronnes (d. ca. 1325), in *Quodlibet 7*,[11] tries to defend this position more for the sake of disputing than asserting; and a certain Bernadine Mirandulanus [Antonio Bernardi della Mirandola (1503-1565)], does defend it in his *Exposition of the Categories*.[12] The basis [of this position] can be that something is called a being of reason either because it is in reason as in a subject or because it is made by reason. But neither will do, because "to be in" and "to be made" are properties of real beings. Hence it is evident that acts and species[13] which are made by reason and exist in it are real beings. Or something is said to be a being of reason because it is made up (*fictum*) by reason, and since what is merely made up does not exist, to say that it does exist involves a contradiction. Or at least (which is more to the point) it follows that such beings of reason are not in any way needed, either for disciplines (*doctrinas*) or for conceiving true things; for intellectual fictions are not necessary for those purposes.

---

11. Cf. *Praeclarissima ac multum subtilia egregiaque scripta illuminati doc. F. Francisci de Mayronnis ordinis Minorum in quatuor libros Sententiarum. Ac quolibeta eiusdem, ...,  Quodlibetti Questio VII* (ed. Venetijs, 1520), fol. 238v.-241r. For some of what was involved for Mayronnes in this, cf. E. Gilson, *History of Christian Philosophy in the Middle Ages* (New York, 1955), p. 768, n. 74.
12. Cf. *Institutio in universam logicam* (Basileae, 1545; Romae, 1562). I have not been able to see this work.
13. That is, "expressed species."

## A Second Opinion:
## Giving Beings of Reason a True Character of Being.

3. A second, completely opposite, opinion is that not only are there beings of reason, but they also are contained under the common appellation of being with a single signification or even conception, although according to an analogous likeness. Indeed, there are those (whose opinion we have refuted above),[14] who posit a univocal likeness between some beings of reason and some real beings, for example, between relations. There are also some who attribute to beings of reason an entity independent of the actual knowledge of the intellect. Their opinion touches upon the question of the manner in which beings of reason arise or are caused (by the intellect), and accordingly we will treat it better in the following section. The foundation, therefore, of this opinion can be the fact that beings of reason (for example: *blindness* and similar things) are without qualification said to be. Thus, they somehow agree with real beings in the character of being. Likewise, [this opinion has as its foundation] that the attributes of being belong to beings of reason; for a being of reason is one or many, and it is intelligible,[15] etc.

### The True Opinion.

4. *Beings of reason must be granted.* – But it must be said that there are some beings of reason – which are not true and real beings, because they are not capable of true and real existence, nor do they have any true likeness with real beings, by reason of which both would share a common concept of being. The first part of this assertion is standard (*communis*), as is clear from ordinary usage and the way of speaking both in theology and in philosophy. It is also clear from the above treated distinction concerning real relation and relation of reason;[16] for a relation of reason is a being of reason. Aristotle also, in *Metaphysics*, Book V, text 14,[17] has distinguished two kinds of being: one which is truly in reality and another which is not always in reality, but only in the mind's apprehension. For example, when we say a man is blind, that "is" does not indicate some thing which is in the man; rather, by the addition of such a predicate

---

14. See *DM* 47, sec. 3, nn. 2-5; XXVI, 794-795, where, in paragraph 2, Suárez has named his opponents as Cajetan, Capreolus, Deca, Ferrara, and Soncinas – all of them Thomists.
15. On this, cf. note 3, above in the Prologue.
16. Cf. *DM* 47, sec. 3, nn. 2-5 (XXVI, 794-796).
17. Cf. *Metaphysics* V, c. 7; 1017a 32ff.

something is removed from that man. Nevertheless, because the intellect apprehends that lack of sight in the manner of being (*per modum entis*), it says it is in the man – which "is" signifies the truth of the proposition, not existence in reality. And thus from this passage St. Thomas and other expositors infer [that Aristotle is talking about] beings of reason. In the same way Aristotle again, in *Metaphysics*, Book IV, text 2,[18] numbers negations and privations among those things which are in some way called beings. This will be more evident from what we will say below about the divisions of being of reason.[19]

5. *The Division of Being of Reason to be Considered*. – This part cannot be confirmed by argument unless first we explain what sort of being (*esse*) and what sort of essence (*essentiam*) this being of reason, about which we are speaking, possesses. But since being of reason, as the term itself indicates, entails a relation to reason, it is right and usual to distinguish a number of beings of reason according to diverse relations (*habitudines*). For there is a certain kind of being, which is effected by reason, with a true and real efficiency. In this way, all artifacts can be called beings of reason inasmuch as they are made through reason. However, this way of speaking is not usual, because, merely on account of a relation to an efficient or an exemplar cause, an effect is not customarily designated in such a singular way. Of another sort is a relation to reason as to a subject of inhesion, and [this] is a more proper denomination inasmuch as an accident is said to be "of the subject" in which it is, for an accident is "a being of a being" (*ens entis*). And so all perfections which inhere in the intellect, whether they are made by it or whether they result or are infused [into it] from elsewhere, can be called beings of reason. But we are not now talking of these, for they are true and real beings, contained under the categories of the accidents previously expounded.[20] Hence, that understanding of being of reason is not very usual, because reason in this relation is considered too much like a material cause (*valde materialiter*).[21] Therefore, something is said to be in reason in another manner by way of being an object. For inasmuch as knowledge comes about through a certain assimilation and, as it were, a drawing of the thing known to the knower, the thing known is said to be in the knower not only as inhering

---

18. Cf. *Metaphysics* IV, c. 2; 1003b 8-11.
19. Cf. *Section* III.
20. Suárez is referring to earlier *Disputations* 39-53 (XXVI, 504-1014).
21. Two points on this: (1) as Suárez understands it, a being of reason does not inhere in a subject; and (2) in *Section* 2, n. 1, below, he will deny that a being of reason itself has a material cause.

through its image but also objectively in its own right (*secundum seipsam*).[22]

6. But that which is in this way objectively in the mind sometimes has in itself, or can have, true real being, in line with which it is an object for reason.[23] Absolutely and without qualification, this is not a genuine being of reason but rather a real being, for this [true and real] being is what simply and essentially belongs to it; whereas, to be an object for reason is extrinsic and accidental to it. But at times something is an object for reason, or considered by reason, which does not have in itself any other real and positive being besides being an object for the intellect or for the reason thinking of it. And this is most properly called a being of reason. For it is in reason somehow, that is, objectively, and it does not have another more noble or more real way of being from which it could be called being. Therefore, what is normally and rightly defined as a being of reason is *that which has being only objectively in the intellect* or is *that which is thought by reason as being, even though it has no entity in itself*. Hence, Averroes (d. 1198) in *Metaphysics* VI, comment. 3 [sic],[24] has correctly said that a being of reason can have being only objectively in the intellect. And St. Thomas, in *Opuscule* 42, chapter 1,[25] says that a being of reason is produced at that point when the intellect tries to apprehend what is not and then fashions it in some manner as being. He also indicates the same in *Summa theologiae* I, q. 16, 3, ad 2;[26] and in I-II, q. 8, 1, ad 3,[27] he says, that "that which is not in [extra mental] reality is taken as a being in reason." In the same way, [Paul] Soncinas (d. 1494) in *Metaphysics*, Book 10, chapter 5 [sic],[28] [Thomas del Vio] Cajetan (1469-1534) in [his

---

22. The allusion here is to the distinction between the formal concept and the objective concept. On this distinction, cf. esp. *DM* 2, s. 1, n. 1 (XXV, 64-65). On the equivalence of image and formal concept, cf. *DM* 2, 1, n. 11 (XXV, p. 69); also see Suárez, *De Trinitate* IX, 8, n. 4 (I, p. 744); *ibid*. n. 9 (p. 745).
23. On this actual or possible being which is distinct from and more than a being of reason, cf. my articles, "Suarez on the Reality of the Possibles," *The Modern Schoolman*, XLV (1967), esp. pp. 40-42; and "Suarez on the Analogy of Being," *The Modern Schoolman*, XLVI (1969), esp. pp. 331-333.
24. Cf. Averroes, *In Libros Metaphysicorum Aristotelis*, l. VI, c. 2, comm. 8; ed. Venetiis apud Junctas (1574), VIII, p. 152.
25. See *De natura generis*, c. 1, in *S. Thomae Aquinatis, Opuscula omnia necnon opera minora*, ed. R. P. Joannes Perrier, O.P. (Paris, 1949), p. 495. This work is regarded by James Weisheipl (*Friar Thomas D'Aquino: His Life, Thought, and Work* [New York, 1974], p. 403) as "of uncertain authenticity."
26. See Leonine edition, Tome IV (1888), p. 210.
27. Cf. *Ibid*., Tome VI (1891), p. 69.
28. For this cf. Pauli Soncinatis, O.P., *Quaestiones metaphysicales acutissimae* (ed. Venetiis, 1588), In L. IV, q. 5 (p. 10).

commentary on] *De Ente et essentia*, chapter 1,[29] and Durandus [of Saint-Pourçain (ca. 1275-1334)] in I *Sent.* d. 19, qu. 5, n. 6,[30] and qu. 6, n. 9,[31] and d. 33, qu. 1, n. 10,[32] explain the nature of a being of reason. Durandus, however, adds that the whole being of a being of reason is an extrinsic denomination from an act of reason – which addition is equivocal and contains a difficulty that will be treated in the following section.

7. Therefore, from this clarification of the term, which is also a definition of the thing signified (as far as it can be [so defined] at this place) it seems one may clearly infer that there is given something which can be called by that title, "a being of reason." For many things are thought by our intellect which do not have real being in themselves, although they may be thought in the manner of beings, as is clear from the examples brought up of blindness, a relation of reason, etc. Likewise, many things are thought which are impossible, and are fashioned in the manner of possible beings, for example, a chimera, which does not have any other being besides being thought.[33] Again, this very thing we are doing, in disputing about being of reason, does not come about without some thinking of that [being], and through reflection we also conceive ourselves to be disputing about a certain kind of being which in itself does not truly exist. Therefore, unless he does not know what he is saying, no one can deny that there is given something of this kind fashioned by thinking alone, unless perhaps he is laboring under an equivocation in the use of the words "to be given" or "to be." For when we say there are given or there are beings of reason, we do not understand them to be given or to be with real existence in [extra mental] reality; otherwise, we would be involved in a contradiction in terms. Hence, if they who deny that there are beings of reason only mean to deny this, they do not contradict us. But they are not here speaking in accord with the subject matter. For beings of this kind are said to be given or to be – not without qualification, but to a certain extent (*secundum quid*), according to their capacity, that is to say, only objectively in the intellect, and in this way the

---

29. Cf. Thomae de Vio, Caietani, O.P., *In De Ente et Essentia D. Thomae Aquinatis, Commentaria*, cura et studio P.M.-H. Laurent, O.P. (Taurini, 1934), p. 23.
30. Cf. D. Durandi a Sancto Porciano, Ord. Praed. et Meldensis Episcopi, *In Petri Lombardi Sententias Theologicas Commentariorum libri IIII* (ed. Venetiis), 1571, p. 66r.
31. Cf. *Ibid.*, p. 66v.
32. Cf. *Ibid.*, p. 89r.
33. Admitting "impossibles" as beings of reason, Suárez is aligning himself with Averroes [cf. *In Metaphy.* VI, c. 2, t. 3; ed. Venice, 1562, f. 152], for whom the core of Aristotle's "being as true" is to be found in such items. Against this, cf. e.g., Duns Scotus [*Quodl.* III, a. 1; ed. Alluntis (Madrid, 1968), pp. 93-94], who excludes such items from any and all intelligibility.

matter is clear. We will explain the manner of this existence more in the following section.

**Why Beings of Reason are Contrived.**

8. Secondly, from what has been said, one may infer the source or the occasion for fashioning or contriving beings of reason of this sort. Indeed, three sources can be given. First, there is the knowledge which our intellect tries to pursue concerning those negations and privations which are nothing. For since being is its adequate object, our intellect can conceive "nothing" only in the manner of being, and therefore when it tries to conceive privations or negations it conceives them in the manner of being.[34] St. Thomas, in the passages cited, touches upon this reasoning – which does not seem to apply in the case of relations of reason. Hence, there needs be added a second cause deriving from the imperfection of our intellect. For since it sometimes cannot know things as they are in themselves, the intellect conceives them by comparison with one another, and in this way forms relations of reason where there are no true relations. For just as, inasmuch as it cannot by a single concept distinctly know the whole perfection of one simple thing, it divides it up with different concepts and thus forms a distinction of reason, so also, when it compares things which in reality are not related, it forms a relation of reason. But [the intellect] often needs such comparing, because it cannot conceive a thing as that thing exists in itself, or indeed (*certe*) because it wants to explain in a manner fitted to its own self what exists in reality without such a manner, as when it predicates one thing of itself, saying it is the same as itself. But these two [sources or occasions] (*modi*) are founded somehow in [extra mental] things, or they are ordered to knowing something which can truly be said about those things. However, there is a third cause resulting from a certain fecundity of the intellect, which can construct figments from true beings, by uniting parts which cannot be combined in reality. In this way, it fashions a chimera or something similar, and thus it forms those beings of reason which are called "impossibles" and are said by some to be "prohibited" beings.[35] In these conceptions, however, the intellect is not in error, since it does not affirm those things

---

34. For being as the adequate object of our intellect, see Suárez, *De Anima* IV, c. 1 (III, 713-715). For the exclusion of beings of reason as such from this object, cf. esp. *ibid.*, n. 4 (p. 714).

35. See note 33, above. For the term "prohibited" beings as equal to impossible beings, cf. Francis of Mayronnes, *Quodl.* VII, n. 7; fol. 239v.

to be such in reality as it conceives them by a simple concept – in which there is no falsity. And thus we have sufficiently answered the arguments of the first opinion.

**What is Common to Beings of Reason and to Real Beings.**

9. Thirdly, from what has been said against the second opinion, it is easy to show that, although it in some way shares the *name* of being (and not just equivocally and as they say "by chance," but rather through some analogy and proportionality to true being), a being of reason cannot however share or agree with real beings in the *concept* of being. The first part is evident from Aristotle, in *Metaphysics*, Book IV, at the beginning,[36] where he asserts the analogy of being with respect to privations and negations. Similarly, in Book V, chapter 7,[37] he counts beings of reason in the division of being. But in that book he is not distinguishing merely equivocal terms. Moreover, as is clear from what has been said, a being of reason is called being only because it is fashioned and thought in the manner of being, as is very obvious in relations of reason. In the same way, a distinction of reason is called a distinction because of some proportion to a true and real distinction, or because in some way it is founded on a distinction of concepts which the intellect makes. Finally, that which according to no disposition (*habitudo*)[38] or proportion can be compared to a true being can be called neither a being of reason nor a being in any way. Therefore, being is not said of a being of reason except through some analogy, at least of proportionality, or some reference (*habitudo*), i.e., because it is in some way founded on being or refers to it.

10. *No Common Concept can be Assigned to Real Beings and Beings of Reason.* – However, a common concept has no place here, because a concept of this kind requires that the form signified by the term be truly and intrinsically shared by the inferiors. But "to be" (*esse*), from which something is called a being (*ens*), can not be intrinsically shared by beings of reason. For to be only objectively in reason is not to be, but rather to be thought or to be imagined. Hence, the usual description, as it can be given with respect to the common concept of being, namely, that which has being (*esse*), does not in fact fit beings of reason. Therefore, they cannot be said to have an essence. For an essence, said without

---

36. Cf. *Metaphysics* IV, c. 2; 1003b 8-11.
37. Cf. 1017a 18 and 32ff.
38. The term, *habitudo*, will become more pointed in *Section* II, n. 10, below.

qualification, entails a relation (*habitudo*) to being, or a capacity for that. But a being of reason is such that being cannot belong to it. From this there also arises a difference between an accident and a being of reason. For an accident, absolutely and without addition can be called a being, since although it is analogically a being, it is still properly and intrinsically a being.[39] A being of reason, however, cannot be called being absolutely, but only with some addition, which makes it plain that it is not a true being, but rather thought in the manner of a being. This is confirmed: for a being of reason is farther away from a real being in the character of being than a man in a painting is from a true man. For in this latter case there is at least a real likeness in some accidental feature, which cannot in any way exist between a real being and a being of reason. *You may say*: by a similar argument it would be proven that there cannot be an analogy of proportionality here, for neither can a being of reason have a proportion with a real being. *The answer is*: although a being of reason as such does not have in itself a proportion or the foundation of a proportion, for in itself it is nothing, nevertheless, it is thought in the manner of having a proportion or a relation (*habitudo*), and this is enough to found some analogy, as St. Thomas has taught, in *De Veritate*, qu. 2, a. 11, ad 5.[40]

## Section II.
## Whether a Being of Reason Has a Cause, And of What Kind That May Be.

1. *There is no final cause of a being of reason. – Also no formal cause. Nor is there any material cause.* This question can be understood only about an efficient cause. For since it is not something which is directly (*per se*) intended by nature or by any agent, a being of reason cannot of itself (*ex se*) properly have a final cause. If, however, on the part of a man contriving or fashioning beings of reason, some final cause (*ratio*) can be offered, that is more the final cause of that man's thinking than of the object made and thought. And that final cause (*finis*) has been sufficiently explained in the preceding section.[41] Again, since a being of reason is

---

39. On the intrinsic analogy of being between substance and accident, see my article, "Suarez on the Analogy of Being," *The Modern Schoolman*, XLVI, n. 3 (March 1969), esp. pp. 236 and 241.
40. See Leonine edition, Tome XXII, Vol. 1 (1975), p. 80.
41. Cf. *Section* I, n. 8.

itself fashioned in the manner of a certain form, e.g., a relation or something similar, any other formal cause for it is unnecessary. Finally, since it is not in any thing as in a subject, but, as was said, only in the intellect as an object, it also does not have a material cause. However, if a thing which is denominated as a being of reason is considered in the manner of a subject, it could be called the matter or the quasi-matter of that denomination or form. Consequently, if that thing so denominated is considered as something synthesized by reason, it could be said to have a formal cause, namely, the being of reason itself taken abstractly (*in abstracto*). For example, when man is called a species, that concrete species [i.e., the species "man"] is a certain being of reason, whose matter [i.e., content] is man, but whose form is the relation of species. This, however, needs to be explained according to various opinions, and also for various beings of reason, in diverse ways, in line with what we will say below.

**The First Opinion about the Efficient Cause of Beings of Reason.**

2. Therefore, we need to speak about only the efficient cause. To be sure, some simply deny this cause for beings of reason. Soncinas has felt this way in his *Metaphysics* VI, qu. 18,[42] although he does not say absolutely that they have no cause, but that they have no cause giving them being. In addition, he is evidently speaking about the being of existence (*esse existentiae*); in which sense the matter is most clear, since it has been shown that a being of reason has being only as an object in the intellect. However, as I have said above,[43] these questions must be understood according to the subject matter, and therefore, supposing what we have said about the nature of a being of reason, it is pointless (*ineptum*) to inquire after a cause which may through a real efficacy give it being, whether mediately or immediately. However, since a being of reason does not always exist in the way in which it can be, but may sometimes begin to be in that same proportional way, it is not pointless to ask for a cause of this [beginning] to be, of whatever kind it is, of such a being (*hujus qualiscunque esse talis entis*).[44]

---

42. Cf. *Quaestiones metaphysicales* . . . , In L. VI, q. 18, esp. p. 127.
43. Cf. *Section* I, n. 7.
44. On this, cf. paragraph 3, immediately following.

## The First Assertion.

3. *There is an Efficient Cause of a Being of Reason, and how [this Cause] operates (et quomodo illud attingat).* – First, then, it must be said that there is some efficient cause from which a being of reason in its own way derives its being. Yet, its causation (*efficientia*), as it is a real production, does not terminate at that [being of reason] as at a terminus of production, but only as at the object of the produced term itself.[45] This is proven: for although a being of reason does not have real being (*esse*), it does have objective being. But it does not always have this. Therefore, the fact that it has it now, and not before, must be referred to a cause that is in some way efficient. Otherwise, no sufficient reason for that sort of variation could be given. Again, that objective being, although in the being of reason itself it is nothing, still necessarily supposes some real being, on which it is founded, or from whose denomination or relation (*habitudo*) that objective being, as it were, results. Therefore, that cause which produces such a real being is the cause of the being of reason. Hence, the latter part of the conclusion is easily understood. For such a cause effects something (*aliquid operatur*) through a real causation, as, for example, a certain thinking or imagining, which is something real in the intellect itself. But all that causation is terminated, as at a term of real production, at the formal concept of the mind itself, and it stops there. From that point, however, it follows that this same formal concept terminates in some way, as at an object, at the very being of reason which is thought or fashioned.[46] Thus, finally, this being of reason itself has objective being in the intellect.

## The Second Assertion.

4. *The Intellect is the Efficient Cause of a Being of Reason.* – Secondly, I say: the intellect is the efficient cause of beings of reason. However, it effects them merely by producing some thought or concept[47] of its own, by reason of which a being of reason is said to have objective being in the intellect. This is clear enough from what has preceded, and from the very expression (*appellatio*) "being of *reason*," as it has been explained

---

45. As will be made clear in this paragraph the "produced term" would be the formal concept and its object would be the objective concept.
46. On the distinction involved here between the formal and the objective concept, cf. Suárez, *DM* 2, s. 1, n. 1 (XXV, 64-65).
47. That is, a formal concept.

above.[48] For if a being of reason has only objective being in the intellect, then it has that by means of some act of the intellect for which it is an object. Consequently, through the efficacy of that act it has that being. Therefore, that is called the effecting of that being of reason itself, in a broad way and according to the limit of the subject matter, as we have repeatedly said.[49] Against this assertion, one might offer the opinion that every extrinsic denomination is a being of reason, even before any consideration of the intellect – about which opinion I will presently speak.

**Various Doubts about the Proposed Assertion.**

5. Indeed, about this assertion there are many things to be asked and to be explained. First, what is that action or thinking of the intellect, through the efficacy of which a being of reason is said to result? And consequently, does some being of reason result in its object through any act of the mind, or only through certain determinate acts, and which may they be? Then, [we ask]: whether creating beings of reason in this way is proper to the intellect, or whether it belongs also to the will, or even to the senses, and universally to potencies having proper objects? Finally, [we ask]: whether this must be understood only about the human intellect, or whether beings of reason also result through the divine or an angelic intellect?

**An Opinion Asserting that a Being of Reason Consists in an Extrinsic Denomination.**

6. It is, therefore, an opinion of certain persons that a being of reason is nothing other than an extrinsic denomination, by which a thing known is denominated from the act of intellect according to some property or condition belonging to it insofar as it is known. This denomination can be of different sorts. The first denomination of all seems to be that by which a thing is said to be "known," for this also is an extrinsic denomination resulting from an act of the reason, and it does not apply to the thing, except insofar as it is objectively in the mind. Then there are denominations taken from the various operations of the intellect – as from the first operation: "to be universal," "to be a genus," "to be defined," etc.; from the second operation: "to be affirmed," "to be denied," etc.; from the

---

48. See *Section* I, n. 6.
49. Cf. *Section* I, n. 7 and *Section* II, n. 2.

third: "to be an antecedent," "to be a consequent," etc. For it is the common consensus of everyone that these are all beings of reason, and it is clear because to be so denominated is nothing real in things and, nevertheless, it is conceived and said as if it were something. Again, it is clear because those denominations are equally attributed to non-beings, for a privation also is "known," "affirmed," "denied," etc. And the fact that these denominations are derived precisely from an act of the intellect, by which a thing is known in this or that way, is proven because, precisely from the fact that the intellect knows a thing, that thing is said "to be known." Hence, although the act of understanding in the intellect itself is a true thing intrinsically affecting it, nevertheless, in the object [the designation] "being understood" is only a denomination of the reason, and so it is a being of reason. However, from the fact that the intellect knows a thing in such a way, e.g., abstractly, it is denominated "universal," and so with other [denominations]. And thus explained, this opinion is attributed to Durandus, in I *Sent.*, dist. 19, qu. 5 and 6;[50] but we will see afterwards whether this is what he thought.

7. *The First Inference from the Previously Stated Opinion.*
– In accord with this opinion it follows, first, that beings of reason not only result in their own way in things known by a human or created intellect, but also [in things known] by the divine intellect. For those things are denominated "known" also inasmuch as they are objects for that intellect. Approximately in this way, [John Duns] Scotus (1266-1308) said that creatures from all eternity have been produced by God in being known (*esse cognito*). For, as we repeatedly said above,[51] that being, in the opinion of Scotus, is not the being of existence (*esse existentiae*), nor the being of essence (*esse essentiae*), since the essence of a creature is not the act of [its] being known (*cognosci*), but that which is known. It will, therefore, be a being of reason. It is true that Scotus himself, in I *Sent.* d. 36, qu. un., at the paragraph: *To the second I say,*[52] states that this being is not the being of a relation of reason, but another "diminished" (*diminutum*) and absolute being.[53] However, he does not state whether it should be called a real being or a being of reason.

---

50. Cf. notes 30 and 31 above.
51. See, e.g., *DM* 20, s. 1, n. 30 (XXV, 753-754), *DM* 31, s. 2, nn. 1-2 (XXVI, 229-230), and *DM* 30, s. 15, n. 27 (XXVI, 178).
52. Cf. *Ordinatio* I, d. 36, qu. un; ed. Vat. VI (1963), p. 288, #44.
53. On this, cf. A. Maurer, C.S.B., "*Ens diminutum*: A Note on its Origin and Meaning," *Mediaeval Studies*, XII (1950), 216-222.

8. *The Second Inference.* – It follows, secondly, from the aforesaid opinion, that beings of reason result not only through the intellect but also through the will, and indeed also through vision, as well as through other similar acts. For, from these also, objects are denominated according to some being which is nothing in them, e.g., "being willed" or "being seen." Hence, Scotus in the same way says that creatures are produced by God in being willed through [his] will and in being known through [his] intellect, as is clear from II *Sent.* d. 1, qu. 1.[54] With even greater reason, a thing is said to be "willed" and "loved" in an entirely extrinsic way by the human will, and a thing is said to be "seen" in an entirely extrinsic way by vision. In all these instances, therefore, the rationale and correlation are the same.

9. Thirdly, from the aforesaid opinion it is inferred that not only do beings of reason exist by dint of the acts of vital powers, but they can also arise from other things or dispositions of things. For in those things, anterior to those acts, some extrinsic denominations are found, which posit nothing in them and which, consequently, will also be beings of reason. Of this sort is the denomination by which a column is said to be "left" or "right" for an animal. Likewise, those which accrue to an object from a power as such, as "to be visible" or "audible," are of this sort. Finally, there are all those non-mutual relations which from the side of one extreme are said to be rational or extrinsic denominations from other extremes. Even more, it follows by a similar argument that the denomination of "clothed" from a garment, of "located" from a place, indeed of "agent" from an action, are beings of reason, since the reasoning is the same or proportional. For each such denomination posits nothing in the thing denominated; indeed, it is on this account that it is called extrinsic. Therefore, it also will be as such a being of reason. For what greater obstacle is in these [instances] than in others?

## Not Every Extrinsic Denomination Can Be Called a Being of Reason.

10. These inferences (*corollaria*), then, make it plain, I think, that this opinion cannot be true as regards this general rule: that an extrinsic denomination as such constitutes a being of reason. For if the denomination is taken from a real form, by this very fact it exists in reality and,

---

54. For this, cf. D. Scotus, *Ordinatio* II, dist. 1, q. 1, (ed. Vaticana, 1973) VII, p. 8, n. 15; pp. 18-19, n. 32; p. 21, n. 36.

consequently, it does not belong among beings of reason. The antecedent is clear: for that form has true real being independent of reason. Therefore, the denomination resulting from that form, although extrinsic, is also, nonetheless, real and does not exist only objectively in the intellect, or only through the working and fictionalizing of that intellect. *You may say*: by the very fact that it is only a denomination, it cannot be more than a being of reason, for a denomination is a work of reason.[55] *In reply*: if by denomination one understands the imposition of a denominative name, that indeed is a work of reason. We are, however, not now treating of an imposition of names, for in this way, with respect to the imposition of a denominative name, even an intrinsic denomination is a work of reason. But we are treating of the unions and relations of those things, in which [unions and relations] such denominative names are founded. These are not works of reason. But in an intrinsic denomination there is a real union or identity, or something similar. Moreover, in an extrinsic denomination, which is taken from things themselves, there is a real relation of one thing to another, from which it results that the thing, toward which the relation exists, is denominated in the manner of a terminus of the relation of the other thing. Under "relation" (*habitudo*) we are including both categorical and transcendental relation.[56]

**A Denomination from an Act of Reason
Is Not Always a Being of Reason.**

11. But if that principle[57] is not universally true regarding an extrinsic denomination taken from real being, neither can it be true as applied to the acts of the intellect, as they directly denominate objects "known." For an act of intellect is just as much a true and real form as the others, and in reality it has a real and transcendental relation to an object, from which it results that the object is denominated "known." *You may say*: this is peculiar to a denomination taken from acts of the intellect, that it can also refer to beings of reason, and thus for a special motive it can be called a being of reason. *But this is not enough*, for the inference from this is only that some extrinsic denomination, even if it is otherwise taken from a real

---

55. For this opinion, cf. Gabriel Vázquez, S.J. (1549-1604), as cited above, *Introduction*, note 44.
56. This clarification of *"habitudo"* is what was alluded to in note 38, above. For Suárez on the distinction between categorical and transcendental relations, cf. *DM* 47, 3, nn. 10-13 and 4, nn. 1-21 (XXVI, 797-805); and also *De Angelis* VI, c. 6, n. 24 (II, pp. 663-664).
57. Cf. paragraph 10, just above.

form, can be extended to beings of reason. But it is not, in opposite fashion, that this denomination suffices to constitute a being of reason. Therefore, as Scotus rightly noted, in the place cited,[58] these extrinsic denominations can be the foundation of some being or relation of reason, if they are conceived as something in the thing denominated. Nevertheless, taken precisely in themselves, they are not properly beings of reason. Moreover, such a foundation is not in the thing itself which is extrinsically denominated, but in another thing from which it is denominated and, hence, it follows that what is conceived in the manner of being in the thing so [extrinsically] denominated is a being of reason.

12. But it can, further, be said to be peculiar to denominations taken from acts of the intellect, that the being which they confer is only objectively in the intellect, which is characteristic of a being of reason, as we stated above.[59] But although extrinsic denominations taken from other things or acts agree with denominations from the intellect insofar as they posit no real being in the things denominated, they differ, nonetheless, insofar as they do not exist only objectively in the intellect and insofar as they are not dependent upon the actual operation of reason. But in this answer two faults are committed. The first is that either emphasis is put only on the term, "being of reason," or one will have to admit other kinds of being which are neither real beings nor beings of reason. This is explained: for if that being which is constituted through an extrinsic denomination from an act of reason has its own character of being, quite distinct (*condistinctum*) from real being, therefore, also a "seen" being or a "loved" being, and in general any extrinsically denominated being, will have as such a certain character of being, distinct from real being. For, as has been shown,[60] there is here proportionately the same reasoning (*eadem ratio et proportio*).[61] But if stress is put on the term, "being of reason," which seems to signify a peculiar dependence upon an act of reason, with no effort at all we can produce many similar or proportionate terms, such as, "a being of imagination," or "[a being] of sense," or "[a being] of will," etc., all of which will be distinguished from real being on account of the mentioned similarity of the reasoning. But if we pay attention not to the term but to the reality, since in all of these there is the same mode of being, they will agree in the general rationale of a being of reason, not as this signifies a peculiar dependence upon an act of reason, but as it

---

58. See note 52, above.
59. Cf. *Section* I, n. 6.
60. See *Section* II, n. 8, above.
61. Literally: "the same reason and proportion."

signifies a being, distinct from real being, which can be called a being of extrinsic denomination.

13. Secondly, that way out (*evasio*) is at fault, because it is, strictly speaking, false that a denomination taken from a direct act of the intellect has being only objectively in the intellect. For, properly, it has being in the intellect formally rather than objectively.[62] Hence, we must avoid equivocation when we treat of "being known" (*esse cognitum*) or other similar denominations from the intellect. For a "being known" can be that being which is known and which properly is objectively in the intellect. Or "being known" can be that being which a thing is said to have precisely inasmuch as it is known, which by dint of direct cognition is not objectively in the intellect, but is rather formally [in the intellect] from the act by which the thing is known. But it is objectively in the reflex cognition by which the intellect knows itself to be knowing or rather by which it knows the thing to be known. Moreover, although with respect to such cognition that being may be objectively in the intellect, it is not, however, only so. For the form from which that denomination derives is not only objectively in the mind but also in reality itself. Just as when the intellect knows a thing to be loved, that "being loved" (*esse amatum*) is indeed objectively in the intellect, but this is not its total being such that it may, for this reason, be said to be only objectively in the intellect. For in reality itself a certain act of love tends to and terminates at a certain thing, and this is the fact itself of that thing's "being loved."

14. Therefore, if we stay precisely with an extrinsic denomination resulting from a real form and from some relation which is not made up but [which is] true and existing in reality, I do not think it belongs under being of reason. Rather, it is included under the scope (*sub latitudine*) of real being, at least on the side of the denominating form. Hence, if the intellect knows nothing else except that a certain form, for example, sight, has an intrinsic relation to a certain object and terminates at that object, and that, on this basis, that object is extrinsically denominated as "seen," it is conceiving no being of reason. For all these items are truly in reality just as they are known, namely, the thing denominated, the denominating

---

62. Here again the allusion to the formal versus the objective concept is unmistakable. Thus "a being of reason" resulting from the direct act of the intellect would be a formal concept. As such, it would be a quality of the intellect immediately effected by the intellect itself. But "a being of reason" which would result from a reflex or comparative act of the intellect would be an objective concept. It would be "quasi-effected" by the intellect inasmuch as it would be the termination of the formal concept immediately effected. On the direct and the reflex acts of the intellect here, cf. this *Section*, n. 16, below.

form, and, completing the denomination, that union of whatever kind it is, which is rather a real disposition (*habitudo*). And in this regard the argument is the same concerning a denomination taken from an act of the intellect as it directly knows a thing: from this act the thing is said to be known, without any fiction of reason, simply through the real existence of the act of knowing with a real relation to the thing which is denominated "known." All of this will be more clear from what follows.

**The First Assertion Toward a Resolution of the Question.**

15. *A Being of Reason Comes to Be through an Act of the Intellect.* – It must be said, therefore, that a being of reason properly comes to be through that act of the intellect by which something that in reality has no entity is conceived in the manner of a being. This assertion is taken from what was said in the first section,[63] and from all the passages of St. Thomas which we cited there, as well as from the causes and occasions which we enumerated there and which are in us for producing these beings of reason. Secondly, it is proven from what was said against the preceding opinion, for if extrinsic denomination alone is not enough, there remains no other way of explaining this causality of beings of reason. Thirdly, it is made clear from the thing itself (*re ipsa*), and by a certain quasi-induction. Thus, by way of example, blindness (and the same is true of a simple negation) can be conceived in two ways. First, negatively only – by conceiving that in a certain organ there is no power of sight, and in this way there arises no being of reason since nothing is conceived in the manner of being, but only in the manner of non-being. But from this it results that in order to form a simple concept of that blindness, the intellect conceives it as a condition affecting an animal or an organ, just as it also apprehends darkness as a certain disposition of the air. In this instance it is conceiving something in the manner of a being, and since it is not conceiving a real being, then it is properly forming a certain being of reason. Something similar may be conceived in beings of reason which have a foundation in extrinsic denominations, such as the relation of the seen [to the seer], the known [to the knower], etc. For these denominations also can be twofold. First, they may be only extrinsic denominations, and in this way while the intellect directly knows that a thing is seen, insofar as vision existing in the eye terminates at it, it does not through this knowing form or know any being of reason. In a second way, these denominations come to be

---

63. See *Section* I, n. 6, above.

relatively (*respective*) inasmuch as our intellect does not sufficiently conceive something as the term of the relation of another thing to it, but immediately conceives it in the manner of a correlative, and then something is conceived in the manner of a relative being in the thing so denominated. And because that is not a real being, nor a real relation, it consequently turns out to be a being of reason. In this way we have made the matter clear, above in *Disputation* 6, sections 6 and 7,[64] and what I said there about the production of a universal can as such be applied to other relations of reason. There also we specified a way of reconciling the various opinions and sayings of the Doctors[65] about beings of reason of this kind and about the knowledge by which they come to be. And, in line with what was said there, the first opinion treated above could also be explained. This assertion will become more evident from what will be said below, particularly about individual beings of reason.

**The Second Assertion.**

16. *Of What Kind is the Act of the Intellect by which a Being of Reason is Fashioned (fabricatur).* – Secondly I say: the act of intellect by which a being of reason arises is in some way comparative, or reflexive, especially when the being of reason is based upon an act of intellect. This is proven and explained: for that act, by which a being of reason in its proper mode is fashioned and arises, by its nature presupposes another concept of real being, in proportion to which or in imitation of which the being of reason is conceived or formed. For example, in a privation such as darkness, there is supposed some knowledge of light, in order that its removal or negation be conceived by way of an opposite condition. Similarly, in order that a wall be known to be seen, there is supposed a knowledge of some vision that terminates at it, and then there can be conceived in that wall a certain quasi-passion resulting in it from the vision which is directed toward it. Therefore, broadly speaking, the fashioning of a being of reason can be said to come about through reflex knowledge. In this we are extending the term "reflection" to all knowledge presupposing other knowledge, and as it were based on that knowledge, which, generally speaking, is more properly signified by the word "comparison" rather than "reflection." But this reflection is properly found in relations of reason, which the logicians call "second intentions," for in their case a direct

---

64. Cf. Suárez, *Opera omnia*, Vol. 25, pp. 223-231.
65. That is, the Scholastic teachers of philosophy and theology.

operation of the intellect comes first and then there is added a second act, by which some condition in the known subject is considered in the manner of some being existing in it, although in fact there is nothing real but only an extrinsic denomination. So, for example, the intellect first conceives Peter to be white, which is the direct operation, by which the intellect does not fashion or know any being of reason, but only what is in reality – although that manner by which it knows such a fact, namely, by intellectually composing, in the sense of making one thing a subject and another a predicate, is not found in reality. That manner, however, is not, by virtue of that act, attributed to the thing known; nor is it known as something existing in that thing. Therefore, that act is not yet part of the causality of a being of reason, except remotely as a foundation. But afterwards, the intellect reflects and considers the order of those extremes as they are objects for reason's act of composition, and it understands that one is compared to the other as a subject, and the other is compared to it as a predicate. Thus it considers them as being mutually related, although in actual fact such a relation does not exist. And in this way all similar second intentions come about through concepts that reflect upon prior denominations resulting from direct concepts, which, as we have said, do not belong under the proper notion of that being of reason, of which we are now treating. It is necessary only to note (what I have noted above while treating of the universals)[66] that this reflection can take place in many ways. For after the intellect apprehends in the manner of being that which is not truly being, it can again reflect and consider what kind of relation it is that it has fashioned and what terminus it has and the like. Therefore, all this reflection is not necessary in order to understand that a being of reason is fashioned, but as soon as something which is not truly a being is conceived in the manner of a being, a being of reason is understood to be fashioned. And these remarks seem sufficient for the first question[67] and for all that is implied in it.

### A Being of Reason
### Properly Arises Only Through an Act of Intellect.

17. *A Sense Power does not produce beings of reason.* – *The Power of Appetition does not form beings of reason.* – It is, hence, easy to resolve the second question as well.[68] For it must be said that genuine beings of

---
66. Cf. *DM* 6, s. 6, nn. 11 and 12 (XXV, 228).
67. Cf. this *Section*, n. 5, above.
68. Cf. *ibid*.

reason are in no way formed or exist either in the senses, or in the will or appetite. Neither a sense nor an appetitive potency has this power of forming or conceiving in the manner of being that which is truly not being. For a sense is not reflective nor does it, like the intellect, inquire after quiddity, so that it may thereby conceive in the manner of being things which are not beings. This is especially the case inasmuch as *being as being* is not the adequate object of a sense in the way that it is of the intellect.[69] In this regard, the argument is the same for the will, which does not tend to being as being, but as good. And although sometimes the human will tends toward what is in reality not good as if it were good, nevertheless it does not fabricate such good, but it supposes it as apprehended and represented by the intellect. Hence, even if that were counted among beings of reason, it is not fashioned by the will but by the intellect. Nevertheless, even though the will, like the senses, denominates its object as "loved" or "desired" by a real extrinsic denomination through the relation of its act to such an object, still the will itself does not reflect further. It does not inquire what "to be loved" or "to be desired" is in such an object, nor does it fashion a being of reason in that object. This is, rather, the task of the intellect. And although the will could in its own order reflect upon its own act, by loving love or desire,[70] and although it could reflect on the object as denominated by the act of the same or a similar will, namely, by loving the object because it is loved by another, still through this reflection it does not fashion in the manner of being or good anything which is not in itself good. But it tends to each thing as it exists in itself or as it is proposed by the intellect. For this reason, although the will may tend to a universal object, the will as such does not fashion the universal, but presupposes it as fashioned by the intellect. And it is the same with all objects to which the will tends on account of extrinsic denominations or dispositions which, if they are conceived in the manner of relations, are indeed only relations of reason, as when the will loves some act because it is prescribed. For "to be prescribed" is an extrinsic denomination, which, if it is apprehended as something existing in the thing itself that is prescribed, will be a being of reason. However,

---

69. Cf. *Section* I, n. 8, note 34, above.
70. Here it is tempting to think that Suárez might have had St. Augustine in mind; cf., e.g., "To Carthage I came, where there sang all around me in my ears a cauldron of unholy loves. I loved not yet, yet I loved to love, and out of a deep-seated want, I hated myself for wanting not. I sought that I might love, in love with loving..." *The Confessions of Saint Augustine*, Book III, trans. Edward B. Pusey (New York: Random House, 1949), p. 36.

that does not come about through the will, but through the intellect. From these remarks, therefore, it is clear enough that beings of reason are not produced by the will or by the senses.

18. *Whether the Imagination is Productive of Beings of Reason.* – From this general rule the human imagination can be excepted. For it sometimes fashions certain beings which in fact never exist, nor even can exist, by composing them from those beings which are sensed – as when it fashions a golden mountain, which does not exist, although it is possible, and is able in the same way to fashion an impossible thing, such as a chimera.[71] For by the very fact that it has power to combine simple appearances, forming through them an image (*idolum*) consisting of things represented by simple phantasms, just as it can combine those which do not involve contradiction even though *de facto* they may not be found so combined, so also it can fabricate a combination of things whose coherence is contradictory. Hence, the dialecticians also say that imaginable being has a wider extension than possible being.[72] Thus, it must certainly be said that those beings of reason which are merely impossible, and do not have any other foundation in reality apart from a potency's power to combine what in reality cannot be combined, can also be fabricated by the imagination. However, because the human imagination in this case participates somehow in the power of reason, and perhaps never does this without the cooperation of reason, all these things are therefore said to be beings of reason and, speaking without qualification, this task is also attributed to reason.

**Does the Divine Intellect Form Beings of Reason?**

19. *The Opinion of Some.* – Finally, from what has been said, we can deduce a reply to the last question[73] about the divine intellect – whether beings of reason are formed by it. For many think this should not be denied to the divine intellect, inasmuch as it entails a perfection in our intellect and does not necessarily involve any imperfection. For it is a mark of perfection to understand every intelligible. But these beings of

---

71. On this cf. *Introduction*, note 47, above.
72. For two such dialecticians with whom Suárez would have been familiar, see Domingo Soto, O.P., *Summularum*, editio secunda (Salmanticae, 1554), II, c. 13, n. 4 (44v b) and Franciscus Toletus, S.J., *Introductio in universam Aristotelis Logicam* (Coloniae, 1615), II, c. 8 (p. 33). Also, cf. note 182, below.
73. See this *Section*, n. 5, above. Here Suárez seems to run two distinct questions together, i.e., (1) about God, and (2) about angels.

reason are in some way intelligible. Therefore, it belongs also to the divine perfection to understand them. Again, it belongs to the perfection of a knower to know each thing as it is, or such as it is. But while these beings of reason are such that they are not in themselves true beings, they can, however, be thought in the manner of beings. Therefore, it belongs to the perfection of the divine intellect to comprehend them. Accordingly, although they are not beings, to know them in the manner of beings will not be an imperfection in the divine intellect; rather, it is an imperfection of the object itself that it have such manner of entity. This is confirmed, for the need to fashion these beings of reason does not always result from the imperfection of the knower, but [it sometimes results] from the nature and the intrinsic necessity of the things which are to be known. This is clear first of all in cases of negations and privations, for they are known in the manner of being. The reason is that nothing is essentially intelligible except being. Hence, insofar as they are not beings, they lack intelligibility. Thus, in order to be known, they must be conceived in the manner of beings. This reasoning is common to every intellect, and it is not based upon the imperfection of the knower, but rather on the nature of the knowable object. For just as being is the adequate object of the human intellect, it is also proportionately the adequate object of the divine intellect – speaking of an object, whether primary or secondary, at which knowledge terminates.[74] Accordingly, even the divine intellect can conceive something only in the manner of being. Therefore, it will conceive negations and privations in this way. Again, this is clear with regard to relations of reason, since even the divine intellect conceives things as rationally distinct which in reality are not distinct. For it knows the divine Word proceeds through intellect and not through will, and the Holy Spirit proceeds through will and not through intellect. Similarly, it conceives a man to be created through the idea of man, and not through the idea of lion, and vice versa – and so also as regards other things. There are many theologians in favor of this opinion, who treating of the divine ideas, or divine relations, or attributes, ascribe to God both relations of reason and also (by comparison of the same thing with diverse things) distinctions of reason – as may be seen in St. Thomas, *Summa theologiae* I, qu. 15,[75] a. 2, ad 2 and 3;[76] *Contra Gentiles*, I, c. 18 [sic],[77] and in other theologians at

---

74. On God and creatures as the primary and secondary objects in which divine knowledge terminates, cf. *DM* 30, s. 15, nn. 20-26 (XXVI, pp. 176-178). On a terminative object versus a principiative or motive object of cognition, cf. *DM* 31, s. 2, n. 7 (XXVI, p. 231).
75. Here I have taken the Salamanca 1597 (II, 716) and Mainz, 1605 (II, 651) readings in place of the Vivès reading of "19".
76. Cf. Leonine edition, Tome IV (1885), p. 202.
77. Cf. *ibid.*, I, c. 54; Tome XIII (1918), pp. 154-155.

I *Sent.*, d. 35, and 36.[78]

20. *The Opposite Opinion.* – Nevertheless, from another standpoint it seems to contradict the perfection of the divine intellect that it form beings of reason. For a being of reason is not formed except by conceiving in the manner of being that which is not being. However, this results from an imperfection of intellect and contradicts the perfection of divine cognition, which is based on the fact that it most clearly knows each thing as it is. Therefore, beings of reason cannot be formed by the divine intellect. This is confirmed, because it is impossible that the divine intellect conceive spiritual things after the fashion of corporeal things, since that is an imperfect way of knowing. But it belongs to the perfection of the divine intellect that it see spiritual things as they are and not otherwise. Therefore, by a similar argument, it is impossible that the divine intellect conceive things as distinct which in reality are not distinct. For this way of knowing is also imperfect and foreign (*alienus*) [to God]. Therefore, a distinction of reason cannot be made by the divine intellect. Hence, by a similar argument, no other relation of reason can be made by the divine intellect. The argument is the same or proportional, for God cannot understand as related things which are not related, because that way of conceiving would not be proper and by it things would not be conceived as they are. Finally, for the same reason God does not conceive negations or privations in the manner of positive beings, because he would thus conceive them in an improper way and not such as they are. Therefore, no being of reason of any kind can be formed by the divine intellect.

21. As a result, the assumption made in the contrary arguments seems to be false, namely, that the formation of beings of reason does not result from an imperfect way of knowing, or that it is necessary by virtue of the object understood. For every conception of a thing which, from the side of the object or the way of representing, is otherwise than the thing known, is in itself imperfect and does not have that condition by virtue of the object, but from the side of the knower. But I say, "from the side of the object or in [sic] the way of representing" because from the side of the knower and of the act, or of its entity, it is possible that a thing be formed in the knower otherwise than it is in reality because of the greater perfection of the knower. Thus we know material things in an immaterial way, and God knows composite things most simply, and mutable things

---

78. For examples, cf. Duns Scotus, *Ordinatio* I, d. 35, qu. un., n. 32 (VI, 258); n. 54 (264); d. 36, qu. un., n. 44 (288) and Durandus, *In Sent.* I, d. 36, qu. 3, esp. n. 17 (98v.); qu. 4, esp. n. 5 (99v.).

immutably, and potential things through the most pure act, for all these only indicate perfection in that being (*esse*) by which knowledge is completed. However, with respect to the representation of an object, it belongs to the perfection of knowledge that it represent it as it is. And all knowledge which falls short of this cannot fall short because of perfection of knowledge, but because of some imperfection or limitation joined to it. For the perfection of knowledge consists in an adequation with the thing known and, consequently, in the representation of that thing as it is in itself. Hence, the result is that by virtue of the intellect's object, even a terminative object, another way of knowing is never needed. Rather, the object itself demands to be known as it is.

22. And we can see this clearly by reviewing individual objects or beings of reason. For absolute being, as such, does not demand to be known in the manner of something relative. Indeed, even though two things may appear to us as connected between themselves, if they are not in fact related, they will be more perfectly known as they are in themselves and with the connection they truly have, without any real or contrived relation, than if they are known in a relative manner which does not belong to them. By a similar argument, relative being does not demand to be known in the manner of absolute being, and positive being, as such, does not demand to be known in the manner of negative being. Conversely, negative being does not demand to be known in the manner of positive being. This last, however, is harder to understand because a negation has no entity which can be represented through cognition, unless it is fashioned in the manner of a being. But we must observe that perfect knowledge of a negation does not consist in its being represented directly and in the manner of a being. Rather, in most clearly knowing positive beings we know in them that one is not the other or does not contain the other, or that this is not joined to that, apart from another[79] direct representation of a negation or a privation itself. In this way, God knows negations themselves most perfectly, but with a positive act or judgment whereby, most simply intuiting two things, he simultaneously intuits the fact that one is not the other, and is not joined to the other, or even that it cannot be joined to it. For, besides this act, God does not have another act of a different character, by which he apprehends that negation in the manner of a positive being; for this conception is neither necessary for God nor does it pertain to his perfection. But God is said to know those

---

79. Here I am reading *alia* from Salamanca, 1597 (II, 717), in place of *illa* in both the Vivès and Mainz, 1605 (II, 651) texts.

things which do not exist, as well as those which do exist, not because in order to know those things which do not exist, or negations of beings, he needs to know negation in the manner of positive being, but because he clearly and distinctly knows those things which exist, as well as those which do not exist, by knowing and judging about each one what it is or is not. Moreover, the reason is that God does not receive knowledge from things, nor in order to know them does he depend upon their existence, but he equally knows possible things as well as existing things, and future things as well as present things, yet knowing each one to be as it is, or not to be as it is not.

23. *The Last Opinion is Proven.* – *God Knows Beings of Reason Most Perfectly.* – To me this latter opinion seems true and very much consistent with divine perfection. It occurs to me only to add that, although God does not directly (*per se*) and immediately know by forming beings of reason, nevertheless he does most perfectly know those beings of reason, and for this reason beings of this kind can be said to have some being by virtue of divine cognition. For their being is to be as objects in an intellect; if however they are known by God, they are as objects in the divine intellect; therefore, by virtue of the divine intellect, they have the being which is proportionate to themselves. The fact that these beings are perfectly known by God cannot be doubted, because of the reasons stated for the first position,[80] which at least prove this. It can be further explained inasmuch as God comprehends all acts of human imagination and reason. Accordingly, he comprehends all "formal fictions" (if I may say it so) which can exist in these potencies. Therefore, he also knows "objective fictions" which correspond to or are objects for those mental acts.[81] And thus he knows all beings of reason, which can in any way arise through the operations of these potencies.

24. *Someone, however, can say* that, even though God does in that way know beings of reason, that does not suffice for them to be said to be actually in the way they can be, but only that they be said to be possible, or rather imaginable, or able to be fashioned by the human mind. *The answer is*, if this way of speaking is more acceptable to someone, we need not dispute it. For this would be a dispute about a word rather than about the reality. Furthermore, such a way of speaking is not improbable. For since these beings are only fabricated, they are said actually to be in a proper and particular way when they are actually being fabricated.[82]

---

80. See n. 19, this *Section*.
81. Once again, note the distinction between the formal and the objective concept.
82. For other places in which Suárez says that beings of reason exist only when they are actually being known, cf. *DM* 3, 1, n. 10 (XXV, p. 106); *DM* 6, 7, n. 2 (p. 229); *DM* 8, 2, n. 20 (p. 283); *DM* 25, 1, n. 5 (p. 900), and *De Anima* IV, c. 3, n. 26 (III, p. 730).

However, they are not fabricated by the divine intellect, but they are known as able to be fabricated by a human intellect and under that aspect they can rightly be said not yet actually to be. However, if we speak more broadly about any objective being they have, just as they are actually known by the divine intellect, so also they can be said actually to be.[83]

25. *Whether an Angel and One of the Blessed [in Heaven] Form Beings of Reason*. – But from what we have said about the divine and human intellects, we should make a judgment regarding an angelic intellect, or about any created intellect which is perfect and knows in a superior way, for example, the intellect of one seeing God, as such. For insofar as they perfectly know things as they are in [those things] themselves (*in se*), or in their own selves (*in seipsis*), they do not form beings of reason. But if an angelic intellect perhaps understands such things in an imperfect way, and through species or concepts of other things, it can form some beings of reason. For example, in knowing God by natural knowledge, it can know him by some relationship to creatures and form a distinction of reason in him. But we leave the account and the explanation of this to the theologians, since it presupposes a perfect understanding of the angels' way of knowing.

# Section III.
## Whether Being of Reason is Rightly Divided into Negation, Privation, and Relation.

1. This division is common enough and has a basis in Aristotle, Book IV of the *Metaphysics*, at the beginning,[84] where he lists negations and privations among beings, although in actual fact they are not beings. Hence, his decision to so list them is based only on the fact that they are beings of reason. In line with this, in Book V, chapter 7,[85] he afterwards explains that the being (*esse*) of such beings (*entium*) is being only in the sense of true predication and, therefore, by reason of the intellect, and in the same Book, chapter 15,[86] he suggests (*insinuat*) relations of reason. This division is taken also from St. Thomas, *De Veritate*, qu. 21, art. 1;[87] I

---

83. That is to say they have objective being inasmuch as God actually knows them to be thinkable by human intellects.
84. Cf. *Metaphysics* IV, c. 2; 1003b 8-11.
85. Cf. *Ibid.*, 1017a 32ff. Also see, Suárez, *DM* 31, 1, n. 2 (XXVI, 225); *ibid.* 12, n. 45 (297); *DM* 8, 2, n. 16 (XXV, 282).
86. Cf. 1020b 30-33; 1021a 29ff.
87. Cf. Leonine edition, Tome XXII, Vol. 3 (1976), p. 593.

Sent. d. 2, q. 1, a. 3,[88] and dist. 19, qu. 1 [sic], a. 1,[89] and all more recent authors use the same distinction.

**Difficulties regarding the stated Division.**

2. The division raises some difficulty with respect to its sufficiency and also with respect to the distinction of its members. We will speak of the first issue in the following section.[90] But with regard to the second issue, there can in brief be reason for doubt, inasmuch as negations and privations seem to be incorrectly numbered among beings of reason. For they are not something produced by the mind, but truly belong to things themselves, since [e.g.] in actual reality air is dark and lacking light, and a man is not white if he is black. But if these things are said to be beings of reason because they are fashioned in the manner of being, all beings of reason will in this way be certain negations since none are real and true beings and they all intrinsically include this negation. For another reason also, it is unclear why negation and privation are counted as diverse beings of reason, for if they are considered formally and with regard to the lack or the fabrication of being, they are not diverse. Moreover, inasmuch as they may differ by a relation or a connotation of a subject or a receptive potency, they do not differ under that regard in some entity of reason but, as it were, extrinsically in real entity or in relation to real being. Finally, negation and privation are also not conceived as beings of reason without a relation to something else. Therefore, they are not properly (*recte*) distinguished from a relation of reason. The antecedent is evident, for a privation is the privation of something.

**The Division is Explained and Proven**

3. Nevertheless, the aforesaid division has been correctly handed down (*tradita est*). For, without doubt, those three members, conceived in the manner of being, are beings of reason and not real beings. As regards relations of reason, I suppose this from what was said above,[91] about the category of relation (*ad aliquid*), where we showed that some relations are real and others are rational. These latter we said do not in reality have

---

88. Cf. S. Thomae Aquinatis, *Scriptum super libros Sententiarum Magistri Petri Lombardi*, I, d. 2, q. 1, art. 3; ed. R. P. Mandonnet, O.P., T. I (Paris, 1929), pp. 63-72.
89. Cf. *ibid.*, d. 19, q. 5, a. 1; ed. Mandonnet, pp. 484-490.
90. See *Section* IV, below.
91. See *DM* 47, sec. 3, esp. n. 5 (XXVI, 795-796).

true being "toward another" (*ad aliud*), but are rather thought as having being "toward another." Hence, such relations do not have real being (*esse rei*) but a being which is fashioned by thinking, i.e., therefore, a being of reason (*esse rationis*). Again, a negation of itself does not entail anything real, since it simply removes something real. But regarding a privation, we must for all this matter suppose that sometimes a form which is less perfect by comparison to a more perfect contrary form is called by Aristotle a privation, for example blackness by comparison with whiteness. However, this is not a true privation, but a positive form; hence, it does not belong to this division. Therefore, a genuine privation is said to be a lack of form in a subject apt to have it; cf. *Metaphysics* Book V, chapter 22[92] and Book X, chapter 7.[93] Hence, of itself and formally, it is also a removal and a non-being, as Aristotle also teaches in *Physics* I, chapter 8.[94] Thus both negation and privation, if they are considered precisely insofar as they are non-beings, are as such neither real beings nor beings of reason, since they are not beings, nor are they considered as beings but as non-beings. In this way they are not something fabricated, and they are said to belong to things themselves, not as putting something in them but as taking something away, as Cajetan noted from St. Thomas in [commenting on] *Summa theologiae*, I, q. 48, art. 2,[95] where St. Thomas has the same opinion, as well as in *De malo*, qu. 1, art. 2,[96] and [John] Capreolus (1380-1444) in *Sent.* II, dist. 34, qu. 2, ad 1;[97] [Francis Sylvester of] Ferrara (1474-1528), in [commenting on] *Contra gentiles* III, chapter 19;[98] and Soncinas, *Metaphysics* Book 10, qu. 15.[99] So we say that privations, such as blindness in an eye, darkness in the air, and evil in human actions, are found in [actually existing] things. In this manner Aristotle posited privation as a principle of natural generation.

4. However, from this negation or removal of entity, and from the manner in which our intellect attributes it to things, not only in negating but also in affirming, it ensues that we conceive these not only negatively

---

92. 1022b 32-1023a 6.
93. 1057a 38.
94. Cf. 191b 16.
95. See *Commentaria in Summam Theologicam*, in ed. Leonina, *Operum S. Thomae*, Tome IV (Romae, 1888), p. 493, n. 3.
96. See Leonine edition, Tome XXIII (1982), p. 11.
97. Cf. Johannis Capreoli Tholosani, O.P., *Defensiones Theologiae Divi Thomae Aquinatis*, II, d. 34, qu. 2, art. 3, ad 1; ed. C. Paban and T. Pègues, II (Turonibus, 1903), pp. 396-397.
98. Cf. *Commentaria in Summam Contra Gentiles*, ed. Leonina, Tome XIV (Romae, 1926), pp. 44-45.
99. Cf. *Quaestiones metaphysicales . . .*, L. 10, q. 15; p. 277.

but also in the manner of positive being. Thus conceived, they have the character of a being, not a real being, but a being of reason, as St. Thomas correctly noted in *Metaphysics* IV, chapter 2,[100] where Aristotle has the same opinion. The first point is clear because in this affirmation, "A man is blind," there is virtually included the predication of being, for the verb "is" includes the participle, "being." It is clear also because our intellect does not conceive anything as existing in reality unless it conceives it in the manner of a being. The second point is also evident, because in this mode of conception or affirmation there is no admixture of falsity or deception. For statements of this kind are entirely true; hence, they are also found in the Sacred Scripture, e.g., in *Genesis*, chapter 1: "And darkness was on the face of the deep,"[101] and *John*, chapter 9: "He was blind from birth." Therefore, this being is not ascribed as positing some entity in reality; hence, [it must be regarded] as a being of reason only. For, to be sure, that which in reality is only a deficiency is conceived and attributed to a subject as something existing in it – in which there is indeed an extrinsic or improper[102] way of conceiving or predicating, but still not falsity. Thus, it is clear that those three members are encompassed under being of reason.

**The Difference Between a Relation of Reason and the Other Two Members.**

5. But that a relation is diverse[103] from the other two things encompassed within this order is clear first from the diversity of their foundations. For the foundation which the intellect has for conceiving a relation of reason is not some negation or removal of entity. Rather, it is some positive entity which is conceived by us only imperfectly in the manner of a relation. *You may say*: in order to conceive a relation of reason, there is always presupposed in reality the lack of a real relation. For if a real relation were present, the relation of reason would not be fabricated. *My answer is*: it is true that a lack of this kind or a negation is presupposed as a necessary condition, but not, however, as the proper foundation of the

---

100. See St. Thomas, *In XII Libros Metaphysicorum* . . . , ed. Cathala, p. 152, nn. 539-540.
101. On the negative character of darkness in this verse, cf. also St. Augustine, *De Genesi contra Manichaeos*, c. IV, n. 7, ed. Fr. Balbino Martín Pérez, in *Obras de San Agustin*, XV (Madrid: Biblioteca de Autores Cristianos, 1957), pp. 368-370.
102. That is to say, "metaphorical." On this, cf. *Introduction*, n. 47, above.
103. That Suárez literally means the sharper "diverse" and not just "different" will be clear from what follows. On "diverse" as distinct from "different," cf. *DM* 7, 3, n. 6 (XXV, 273).

relation of reason. Hence, a relation of reason is not fabricated in order to conceive the negation or the lack of a relation[104] in the manner of a positive being, but in order to conceive something else which is positive and absolute in reality, but so connected with another thing that on this account we conceive it in the manner of something relative.

6. Furthermore, from this is derived the proper and formal difference between a relation of reason and the other two members. A relation of reason formally contributes (*dat*) a denomination [which is] relative according to reason, and through that we explain something positive in reality, especially when such a relation has at least some remote foundation in reality itself. I note that in this way, because sometimes [the relation] is founded only on our manner of conceiving, and then it is possible that through it there may be expressed some negation on the side of reality, as is evident from the rational relation of the identity of one same thing with itself.[105] However, this is, as it were, accidental to the relative denomination which a relation of reason as such contributes. But negation and privation, by virtue of their genus, denominate in the manner of something absolute and positive according to reason, although through that denomination we may be expressing only a lack. For example, we denominate air as dark, through which we express a lack of light as if the air were affected by a certain absolute disposition contrary to light.

7. It does not matter that a privation is known through something positive and is defined by way of a relation [to that something].[106] For that results from the negative foundation itself, which is supposed in reality, rather than from the way of conceiving such a being of reason in the manner of something positive. Moreover, the manner of a privation's relation to its corresponding form, as it can be or be conceived in the privation, is not that of a "relation according to being" (*relatio secundum esse*) but of a "relation according to being said" (*relatio secundum dici*),[107] just

---

104. Here the reading of the Vivès edition is preferable to those of Salamanca, 1597 (II, 719) and Mainz, 1605 (p. 652), which run: "*ipsam relationem seu carentiam negationis*" ("the relation itself or the lack of negation").
105. Cf. *Section* VI, n. 5, below. Also see *DM* 7, s. 3, nn. 2-5 (XXV, 272-3).
106. Cf. n. 2, this *Section*.
107. For Suárez a "relation according to being said," which is not identical with a relation of reason, occurs when we conceive or explain something only by way of a relation even though in reality it is not related; cf. *DM* 47, s. 3, n. 6 (XXVI, 796). For example, the divine omnipotence, which is itself absolute, is something relative according to being said. For we cannot conceive of it, nor explain it, except concomitantly with creatures which are its objects; cf. *ibid.*, n. 8 (796). In opposition to this, a "relation according to being" may be either a real relation or a relation of reason; *ibid*. Its distinguishing feature is that, more than simply a matter of our conceiving or speaking, its proper being (real in the case of a real relation, fabricated in the case of a relation of reason) involves a relation to something else; *ibid.*, n. 6.

as one contrary is known through another.[108] Thus there can be a privation of a real relation which is not conceived in the manner of a relation, even though it could not be known without a terminus. So, for example, "to be an orphan" is a kind of privation which seems immediately to deprive one of the relation of sonship, which is taken away by the death of a father, and thus that privation cannot be sufficiently understood without a father. Yet, it is not conceived in the manner of a relation, but rather in the manner of a certain absolute disposition which remains in one extreme when the other is taken away. For, by the very fact that we express the privation of a relation by conceiving it in this way, we conceive it in the manner of something absolute, and not relative.

**The Difference between Negation and Privation.**

8. Finally, with regard to the distinction between the two other members, namely, privation and negation, there is no doubt that they are in some way distinct. For privation expresses a lack in a naturally apt subject, but negation expresses a lack in a subject absolutely and without qualification. But whether the difference is essential, i.e., formal, or not, is a question of small importance which we will more fittingly answer in *Section 5*. Now I only note, from St. Thomas, *De malo*, qu. 3, art. 7,[109] that negation can be taken in two ways. First, *in general*, and in this way it is properly and adequately distinguished from a relation of reason and is further divided into what is properly called privation and negation taken more strictly, inasmuch as this expresses a lack not in an apt, but rather in a non-apt subject. And this is the second way in which negation is usually taken. Thus the three-membered division which we are treating contains a pair of two-membered divisions: the first is a division of being of reason into positive, which is relation (*ad aliquid*), and negative. And this first division is into members essentially diverse, in the way, that is, by which in these beings of reason we can think of an essential nature or diversity.[110]

9. *A Reply to a Small Doubt (Dubioli satisfit).* – One can, however, doubt whether this division is univocal or analogous. And if it is univocal, is it a division of genus into species, or of what sort is it? But these matters, which are of little importance, I leave to the discussion and

---

108. On the difference between contrary opposites and relative opposites, cf. *DM* 45, s. 1, n. 8 (XXVI, 739-740); *ibid.*, s. 2, n. 18 (745-746).
109. See Leonine edition, Tome XXIII (1982), pp. 80-81.
110. Of course, strictly speaking they have no essences.

thinking of the reader. To me, indeed, it seems to be univocal, since there is no sufficient reason for an analogy. Again, it seems to be a division of a genus into species. For these considerations (*respectus*) can also be attributed to beings of reason, and in them there can be thought a composition of genus and difference, as I suppose from logic. And in the present instance, the concept of a being of reason can be so abstracted that in its own order it may be conceived as something complete and having differences outside its nature (*rationem*).[111] The second division, or rather subdivision, is of negative being of reason in general, into negation, taken in the strict sense, and privation. We will more appropriately explain this in the two following sections.

## Section IV.
## Whether Being of Reason is Sufficiently Divided into Negation, Privation, and Relation.

1. One reason for doubting [the sufficiency of this division] is that being of reason can be divided proportionately through all the categories; therefore, it is not sufficiently contained in these three members. The antecedent is evident. For, if we review all the categories, in each of them, by proportion with real beings, there are fashioned some beings of reason, which can be the basis proportionately for just as many categories of reason. For example, in the category of *substance*, there is conceived a chimera or similar monsters of reason, which are conceived in the manner of substance inasmuch as they are not fabricated as attributes of other things but imagined as beings by themselves. In the category of *quantity*, first there seems to be imaginary space, which we conceive as a kind of extension; and also that quantity which we conceive, for instance, in a chimera is a being of reason. Again, in *quality*, beings of reason seem widespread. For example, we conceive reputation and honor as a disposition belonging to the person who is honored or who has a good reputation, even though in that person it is only a being of reason. Again, human

---

111. In this place Suárez allows more unity to being of reason than he does to real being, which he refuses to regard as a genus having differences outside its nature; cf. *DM* 2, 5, n. 10 (XXV, p. 96); *DM* 28, 3, n. 20 (XXVI, p. 20); *DM* 30, 4, n. 32 (p. 85); and *DM* 32, 2, n. 15 (p. 322). There is question about these "differences." Just what are they? Beings of reason? Hardly. Real beings? Not likely. Extrinsic denominations? Perhaps. But then, in view of what Suárez has said (cf. *Section* II, n. 10, above) regarding the reality of such, the question is reinstated.

dominion (*dominium*),[112] or jurisdiction, are conceived as certain powers (*potestates*), which are therefore usually called "moral powers" (*potentiae*);[113] however, they are beings of reason. Then, just as we fashion a chimera, so in it we can imagine its distinctive figure, which as such will also be a certain quality of reason. And in almost the same way, the other categories can be fabricated as beings of reason in a chimera. For example, someone might think it to have its own *actions* or *passions*, or modes,[114] and its own *place*, and the like. Moreover, an action especially, if it is conceived as an absolute form inhering in an agent, is a kind of being of reason not in the manner of relation, but in the manner of action. Conversely, denominations of "seen," "known," "loved," and the like, if they are conceived as something in the thing denominated, are each conceived in the manner of a certain passion, and as such they are beings of reason. Likewise, in the category of *time* (*quando*), we conceive an imaginary extension, or a denomination from an extrinsic time as measuring,[115] as though it were something in the thing denominated. And the same is true for the other categories. Therefore, the division of beings of reason is not correctly restricted to those three members. But conversely, unless this division is sufficient, it will be inappropriate to accept it, and that would be contrary to the common opinion.

**The First Way of Explaining the Sufficiency of the Division.**

2. The proposed division can be explained in two ways. The first is that this division should be understood as applicable not to being of reason taken over its whole expanse, but only to that [being of reason] which has some foundation in reality.[116] For, as St. Thomas has noted in *Sent.* I, dist. 2, qu. 1, art 3,[117] and dist. 19, qu. 5, art. 1,[118] there are certain beings

---

112. In different contexts, *dominium* can be political dominion or rule, or it can be mastership, or it can be ownership. All of them would fit the context here.
113. Suárez's main point here seems to be that there are some beings of reason which belong in the second species of the Aristotelian category of quality, i.e., potency; on this last, cf. *DM* 42, s. 3, nn. 9-10 (XXVI, 613); s. 4, n. 7 (p. 617). Also, the Scholastics regularly, but not always, distinguished between *potestas* as power in the sense of moral authority and *potentia* as power in the sense of physical force.
114. On the Suarezian "modes" as they are distributed through the categories, see J. I. Alcorta, *La teoría de los modos en Suárez* (Madrid, 1949), esp. 229-313.
115. For example, in the phrase "yesterday's class," the designation "yesterday's" is extrinsically attached to the term "class" from the measuring motion of the heavens. On this, cf. Suárez, *DM* 50, s. 10, nn. 11-12 (XXVI, 961). Carrying it over, we could easily imagine a chimera to have a duration which would justify speaking of its action as "yesterday's action," etc.
116. Cf. *Introduction*, note 60, above.
117. See note 88, above.
118. See note 89, above.

of reason which have a foundation in things, although they have their completion by the reason, for example, the character of a universal, or a genus, and other like things. Negations and privations are also of this kind, as can easily be understood from what has been said in sections above.[119] But there are other beings of reason which are totally fabricated by the intellect without a foundation in reality, for example, a chimera. Therefore, what is divided in this division can be the being of reason which has a foundation in reality. One can argue for this, inasmuch as a being of reason of this kind is somehow of service to sciences and knowledges of things as they can exist in men.[120] Thus it can fall under science and doctrine. Hence, because the division is doctrinal (*doctrinalis*),[121] it is rightly and exclusively dedicated to that kind of being of reason. For the other kind of being of reason, i.e., merely fictitious, is entirely accidental (*per accidens*)[122] and can be multiplied to infinity. Therefore, no being of reason which has a foundation in reality is fashioned in the manner of substance, but in the manner of an attribute of something, in which it is founded. For every being of reason which is fabricated in the manner of substance is merely fictitious and without foundation. Hence, it is not remarkable that it is excluded from that division. Hence, all beings of reason which are conceived in the manner of an accident in such a fictitious substance are also excluded from this division. For they too are merely fictitious and without foundation. Finally, in line with this interpretation, it can be conceded that beings of reason which are mere fictions range through all the categories, or rather can be framed in imitation of these. But the opposite is true for those beings of reason which have a foundation in reality.

---

119. See *Section* II, nn. 15 and 16; *Section* III, nn. 2, 3, and 4.
120. Think here of scientific constructs such as the epicycles and deferents of Ptolemaic astronomy, which some in the tradition dependent upon Suarez would regard as "beings of reason"; on this cf. above: *Introduction*, note 109.
121. Thus, according to this opinion the beings of reason divided are of use for science and teaching (*doctrina*); also see *Prologue* n. 1, above, and *Section* VI, n. 2, below. In this, they contrast with the other, immediately to be mentioned, beings of reason which can be multiplied to infinity and are of no use for science or teaching; cf. *Prologue*, n. 1 and *Section* I, n. 2, above. Accordingly, the term "doctrinal" as Suárez uses it here and elsewhere suggests a heuristic dimension.
122. An accidental being (*ens per accidens*) would be "one" whose parts would not be properly unified, but instead merely juxtaposed to one another. Unlike categorical accidents, accidental beings would not be true and real beings, see Suárez, *DM* 4, 3, n. 14 (XXV, 130).

**The Stated First Argument for Sufficiency is Examined. –**

3. Following this opinion, however, it remains to be explained why those beings of reason which have a foundation in reality, and which are fashioned in the manner of accidents, cannot be multiplied at least through several categories of accidents. For as I said in the preceding section,[123] being of reason, which is divided into negation, relation, and privation, is basically first divided into positive being and negative being. In order, therefore, that this [threefold] division be adequate, it is necessary that every positive being of reason be also relative. Therefore, we are examining the argument (*rationem*) for this fact. For the discussion in the beginning[124] seems to show that there are many beings of reason having a foundation in reality which are thought in the manner of other categories, especially of quality or potency, of action, and of passion.

4. An argument for this fact [i.e., that every positive being of reason is relative] is usually derived from what is properly constitutive of relation as such, which is "to be toward another" (*esse ad aliud*). For this mode, or quasi-difference, precisely taken, namely, "toward as toward" (*ad ut ad*), of itself does not posit anything inhering in the thing which is related. But absolute [i.e., non-relative] accidents, according to their proper rationales (*rationes*), do entail something inhering. On this account, a being of reason which is conceived as some positive accident may always be conceived in the manner of something relative, and not in the manner of something absolute. For that "being toward another," because it does not of itself entail inhering, can be thought as attached, or as it were joined on, by reason. However, it cannot be thought as something absolute and inhering, because to inhere, from its proper intrinsic concept, expresses something real.[125]

5. This argument seems to have a basis in St. Thomas, *Summa theologiae*, I, qu. 28, art. 1.[126] However, it is necessary to understand and to explain it correctly, for it is difficult in all its parts. First, because "to be toward another," taken truly and properly, is indeed real and inhering, as we have said above,[127] and despite this fact, reason fashions in thought not

---

123. Cf. *Section* III, nn. 8 and 9.
124. Cf. this *Section*, n. 1.
125. To inhere (*inhaerere*) expresses something real inasmuch as to inhere is to exist in (*inesse*) a subject. For Suárez, inherence is a "special mode which is a kind of ultimate terminus of accidental existence"; cf. *DM* 34, s. 4, n. 24 (XXVI, 374).
126. See Leonine edition, Tome IV (1888), p. 318.
127. Cf. *DM* 47, s. 5, esp. nn. 6 and 7 (XXVI, 806-807); and also *DM* 10, 3, n. 14 (XXV, 351).

true, but fictitious, "being toward." Therefore, the same can be said about "being in,"[128] even about absolute "being in." Second, not all the categories of absolute accidents entail true inherence, but some entail an extrinsic adjacency (*extrinsecam adjacentiam*), as was seen above.[129] Therefore, on this account also they contain a basis for being fashioned by the reason. And what Cajetan and other authors think, at that place,[130] namely, that "being toward," as such, abstracts from real being and being of reason (with the result that they base the aforesaid reasoning on this), we have disproved above.[131]

6. Therefore, it seems that argument should be understood as follows. Because a relation according to its proper and peculiar nature includes a disposition not only to a subject but also to a term, the intellect can indeed consider this latter character by itself, not explicitly considering the former, even though in reality this is included in true "being toward." And this separate consideration is enough for the intellect to be able to conceive and compare something as relating to something else, even though such a relation is not truly in it. In this way, there is a peculiar character in relative things, on account of which positive beings of reason can be conceived in the manner of relations. But this character is not found in absolute categories, except perhaps insofar as they include some transcendental relation.[132] For under that aspect they are already in some way "toward another." But if some beings of reason are thought in the manner of relations, they are, by this very fact, fashioned in the manner of categorical, and not transcendental, relations. For, arising through the extrinsic conception of the intellect, those relations are adventitious. Thus, they are not conceived as intrinsically belonging to the essence of some being, which belonging is characteristic of a transcendental relation.[133] But in an absolute accident, insofar as it is absolute, there is no basis for thinking some positive being of reason proportionate to it, whether such an accident be inhering or adjacent. For, in the argument above, an absolute accident should be taken with this whole extension, and the word

---

128. That is, "inherence."
129. Cf. Suárez, *DM* 37, s. 2, n. 8 (XXVI, 494-495); and the whole of *DM* 53 (*De Habitu*) (XXVI, pp. 1011-1014).
130. That is, *Summa Theologiae* I, 28, 1.
131. Cf. *DM* 47, s. 3, esp. n. 4 (XXVI, 795).
132. On the distinction between categorical and transcendental relations, cf. texts cited in note 56, above.
133. Cf. esp. *DM* 47, 3, nn. 11-12 (XXVI, 797-8).

"inhering" itself is sometimes used in that broad meaning. And this argument so expounded will be made more plain by reviewing the individual examples given above.[134]

**Reply to the Difficulties Stated at the Beginning.**[135]

7. *What sort of being of reason is Imaginary Space?* – The first example concerned imaginary space, which we conceive as having dimensions. But, although it is true that space of this kind, when it is so conceived, is a being of reason, it is, however, included under negation or privation taken in a broad sense. For that space, apart from dimensions, is something negative. But, in order to explain it, we conceive it and speak of it as if it were something positive. It is in this, as we have said,[136] that a being of reason which is a negation or a privation consists. From here one can correctly infer that those beings of reason which are negations or privations can be reduced to diverse categories, according to the demands of the forms to which such negations are opposed. This is also the case in that example of imaginary succession, which we conceive apart from real time, for which the same reasoning holds as for imaginary space.

8. Another example concerned certain denominations belonging to the category of quality, such as those taken from reputation or honor which, inasmuch as they are held in human esteem and are appraised as goods, are not proper beings of reason, but rather extrinsic denominations from real forms existing in other things. Thus, honor is said to be in the one honoring, and fame is said to be clear knowledge with praise.[137] But if an occasion is taken from this to fabricate some being of reason in the one honored, this is only in the manner of a relation of an object known, or in another way signified or represented, just as we will say, a little below,[138] about an object seen or known. Another example concerned the moral power of dominion or jurisdiction, and this also is conceived by us in the manner of a certain relation of *superiority*. For, in order to conceive this power we do not fashion or think something in the manner of a quality

---
134. See this *Section*, n. 1.
135. Cf. *ibid*.
136. Cf. *Section* III, n. 4, above.
137. For honor as in the one honoring, etc., see Aristotle, *Eth. Nic.* I, c. 5, 1095b 24-25; St. Thomas Aquinas, *Summa Theologiae* I-II, q. 2, art. 2, ed. Leonina, Tome VI (1891), p. 18 and *Sententiae primi libri Ethicorum*, lect. 5, Tome XLVII, Vol 1 (1969), p. 19. For fame as clear knowledge with praise, see St. Thomas (*Summa Theologiae* I-II, q. 2, a. 3, Tome VI, p. 19) who cites St. Ambrose as its source.
138. See n. 9, this *Section*.

superadded to him to whom such power is given. But we conceive added to him only a relation of superiority founded on some extrinsic denomination resulting from the will of another.

9. A further example was added concerning action and passion, about [each of] which the reasoning is different. For *action*, if it is immanent, is not conceived in the agent as something of reason, but as something real.[139] But if it is transient, either the agent is such that from this action there results in it a real relation, and then from that action there cannot be conceived anything of reason in the agent but only something real.[140] If, however, the agent is such that a real relation does not arise in it, then from such an action there can be conceived something of reason in the agent. That, however, is nothing but a certain relation, because transient action, as such, can be conceived in the agent only in the manner of a relation,[141] for it contradicts its proper nature to be conceived in that agent in the manner of action.[142] *Passion*, however, if it is proper and true, always entails in the thing which undergoes it something which is real and not merely of reason, whether it be considered according to the proper nature of passion, or according to a categorical relation resulting from that. But if something is considered in the manner of a passion, which is not a true passion in a reality, but only according to a way of conceiving and denominating, such as "being seen," "being loved," and the like, then either it is a denomination which is extrinsic and real, or, if it is conceived as quasi-intrinsic and of reason, it is only relative. For it is not really a denomination of a subject of passion as such, but of an object as terminating the act of a potency and as related to that, by the fact that the other [i.e., the act of the potency] is related to it. For in an object or in a terminus so denominated, something cannot be conceived as entirely absolute apart from the denominating act or motion, and therefore it is necessarily conceived in the manner of a relation. This can also be derived from the doctrine concerning non-mutual relatives, offered by Aristotle in *Metaphysics*, Book V, chapter 15,[143] that they are without doubt conceived

---

139. That is to say, immanent action is something really inhering in the agent. To conceive it as such is to conceive it as it truly is, which is not to form a being of reason.

140. The reasoning here parallels that regarding immanent action. The relation in question would be really inhering in the agent. To conceive it as such would be to conceive it as it is. This would not be to form a being of reason.

141. Cf. *DM* 37, 2, n. 14 (XXVI, 497); *DM* 48, 4, nn. 12-18 (XXVI, 891-893); and Suárez, *De SS. Trinitatis Mysterio* VI, c. 2, n. 1 (I, 676).

142. For Suárez's view that action precisely as such is not in the agent, see *DM* 48, s. 4, n. 15 (XXVI, 892). On action and passion as expressing different relations respectively to agent and patient, see *ibid.*, n. 17 (p. 893); and *DM* 47, 4, n. 5 (XXVI, 800).

143. Cf. 1020b 30-33 and 1021a 29ff.

and denominated as correlates to other things (*ad alia*) insofar as [those] other things are related to them. And the same must be said of every denomination of reason founded upon some real extrinsic denomination. For such a denomination is always relative with respect to a denominating form. Hence, if it is not derived from a real relation, it will have to be derived from a relation of reason. Therefore, it is clear that every denomination of reason which is produced in the manner of a positive form, and not in order to conceive or to declare some privation or negation, is produced in the manner of a relation.

**A Second Way to Explain the Sufficiency [of the Division].**

10. The foregoing explanation of this division is suitable enough and it makes the matter clear enough. But we can add another way in which this division is adequate for every being of reason, by including under negation fictitious and impossible beings, whether they are fashioned in the manner of substance or in the manner of accident. For since fictitious beings of this nature are simply non-beings, they are correctly included under negation. Indeed, sometimes in order to explain, by a kind of simple concept, a complex and impossible negation, impossible beings of this sort are fabricated. For example, because it is impossible that a horse be a lion, we say therefore that a being which is conceived in the manner of a horse and lion together (*simul*) is a fiction, and we call it a chimera or something similar. In the same way, in order to explain that this negation is necessary: "An ox cannot fly," we understand a flying ox as something impossible and a being of reason. This appears to be the more common meaning of this division: that all these things are undoubtedly included under negation. Also in this way, adding other points which we made in the previous explanation,[144] it is clearly evident that the division is sufficient, and the fact that beings of reason can be fashioned throughout all the categories does not contradict it. For, besides relations, all the rest are fashioned in the manner of privations or negations.

---

144. Cf. this *Section*, n. 2.

## Section V.
## How Negations and Privations Agree or Differ inasmuch as they are Beings of Reason.

1. We can treat of negation and privation either only insofar as they remove form or positive entity, or insofar as they are beings of reason. For we distinguished these two aspects above,[145] and in accord with them considerations of negations and privations also differ.

**Negation and Privation are Compared as they are in Things.**

2. For, as I suggested above,[146] in negation (and the same is proportionately true about privation inasmuch as it is a removal), if it is a true negation, there is no fabrication by the intellect. Rather, when the intellect conceives precisely that a man is not a horse, it truly conceives what is in reality in the way in which it can be, namely, either positively and fundamentally in the entities of the extremes, or, according to the proper rationale of a negation, by way of removal only. For truly and on the side of reality one is not the other, even if it is not considered or known by any man. But I have said, "if it is a true negation," because if the negation is false, for example, if someone conceives a man who is not an animal, then that negation even under the character of negation is merely manufactured by the intellect, and it has being only as an object in that intellect. Therefore, it is a being of reason, or rather a negation of reason.[147] For that negation, precisely conceived under the character of negation, is also not apprehended in the manner of being, but rather in the manner of non-being, and so it is a certain negation manufactured by the reason. But other negations, which are true, can be called real negations or privations, insofar as they truly remove real forms or natures. Thus, one should not look for a true accidental or substantial essence in them. For they are not said to be [positively] in things as putting something in those things, but negatively, or as removing something from them. Privation and negation

---

145. See *Section* III, n. 4. Suárez will treat negations and privations under the first aspect in paragraphs 2-19, immediately following, and take them up under the second aspect at paragraph 20, below.
146. See *Section* II, n. 22; *Section* III, nn. 2 and 4.
147. Note the parallel between such a "negation of reason" and "relation of reason" or even the alleged "quantity of reason," "quality of reason," etc., considered above; see *Introduction to the 54th Disputation*, G. *Section* IV, above. On a "negation of reason," cf. *DM* 45, s. 1, n. 4 (XXVI, 738).

are, however, beings of reason, insofar as they are conceived in the manner of being, as has been declared above.[148]

## As They are in Things, In What Ways Do Privation and Negation Agree?

3. *The First Agreement. – The Second.* – But leaving out false or fictitious negations, since they neither relate to the present consideration, nor do they require a new exposition besides what was said about falsity in *Disputation 9*,[149] a true and real negation, and a privation, *first of all* agree in this that, with respect to what they entail formally, or as is said, directly (*in recto*), they both consist only in a removal. This is as was said above,[150] and as Soncinas extensively (*late*) treats it in *Metaphysics*, Book 10, question 15,[151] and [Agostino] Nifo (1473-1538), *Metaphysics*, Book 4, Disputation 2,[152] and as is self-evident. They agree, *secondly*, because they are each an extreme of a privative or contradictory opposition which is found somehow in things, and not just manufactured by the intellect. For these oppositions are not contrived by the intellect. And even though they are attributed in a special way to certain acts or composings of the intellect, they still express real opposition among those acts themselves and they also suppose in their objects some opposition, which is not fabricated by the intellect, but is antecedent to all its fabrication, as has been declared above in *Disputation 45*.[153]

4. *Thirdly*, they agree because they both can have a foundation in the thing to which such a negation is attributed, or in one of its conditions, taken absolutely or compared with another. We call a foundation not only the subject to which a negation or privation is attributed, but the proximate cause or root by reason of which such a negation or privation belongs to such a subject. This foundation is seen more frequently and more easily in negation. For, inasmuch as negation does not require a

---

148. See *Section* III, n. 4.
149. Cf. *Opera omnia*, Vivès edition, Vol. XXV, pp. 312-328.
150. Cf. *Section* III, nn. 3 and 4.
151. Cf. *Quaestiones metaphysicales*, In L. X, qu. 15; ed. Venetiis, 1588, p. 278.
152. I am following the readings of Salamanca 1597 (II, 721) and Mainz, 1605 (II, 655), instead of the Vivès reading of "Disputation 3." For Nifo, see: Augustini Niphii, *Delucidarium metaphysicarum disputationum, in Aristotelis decem et quatuor libros Metaphysicorum*, Venetiis, 1559 [reprint: Frankfurt/Main: Minerva, 1967], L. IV, disp. 2, c. 2, p. 105.
153. Cf. *DM* 45, s. 1, nn. 5-6 (XXVI, 739).

subject which is apt to receive an opposite form or nature, it can be based on the intrinsic nature of the subject itself. For example, in man the negation of "apt by nature to neigh" (*hinnibilis*) or "apt by nature to roar" (*rugibilis*), etc., is founded on the intrinsic *differentia* of a man. A privation, however, since it connotes an aptitude in a subject, cannot be founded in that subject as such or in its intrinsic nature alone, but in some other form or added condition. Thus, if a man is blind, that privation is not founded on the precise nature of the man, but in some other cause which removes the form which the privation denies. But this cause is sometimes a positive disposition of the subject. Sometimes it can be a contrary form, as heat in water brings on the privation of cold.[154] But sometimes it is only the absence of an extrinsic cause. For example, in air the cause of darkness is the absence of the sun, although in the air itself there is supposed a nature such that, while it is apt for the form of light, it yet does not of itself have that form. Nor is it of itself necessarily joined to a cause from which it can receive it.

5. *A Fourth Agreement.* – Fourthly, they agree inasmuch as both negation and privation can be truly and absolutely predicated of a thing without any fiction of the intellect. I am not saying without an operation of the intellect, since predication itself is a certain operation of the intellect. But I do say, "without a fiction," because from the side of things themselves there is presupposed basis enough for the intellect to be able to deny one thing of another, conceiving each as it is in itself. Hence, just as the divine intellect or an angel, without any fiction and without composition or division, knows a negation or a privation, so the human intellect without any fiction can know a negation of this kind. But because of its imperfect way of operating, it does this by means of composition or division. For the same reason, it also does it with indirect and as it were discursive knowledge. For this also is common to privation and negation, that they cannot be directly represented through their own species. Therefore, they are known by us indirectly through the species of an opposite form, and by means of some discursive reasoning. Accordingly, knowledge of a privation necessarily presupposes knowledge of a positive thing, through which the intellect could come to know that privation. Thus it is that both privation and negation are known through relation to something positive, by removing that, although by a different act and concept from the act by which the form itself is conceived positively, directly, and

---

154. Note that "cold" is regarded here as a positive quality in much the same way that "blackness" was so regarded in Section III, n. 3, above.

according to itself. Soncinas and Nifo touch upon this in the passages cited above.[155] See also [Chrysostomus] Javellus (d. ca. 1538), *Metaphysics*, Book 10, question 10;[156] Ferrara, *In Contra Gentiles*, I, chapter 71;[157] Capreolus, In *Sent.* II, d. 39, qu. 1, art. 3;[158] and Aegidius [Romanus] (d. 1316), *In Sent.* I, dist. 36, question 2 [sic].[159]

6. We must, however, consider the fact that this [privation or negation] is known by the intellect in two ways. The first is by division or negation, and in this way it is properly known just as it is; for by division one extreme is merely removed from another. The second is by composition or affirmation, as when we say: "The man is blind," or "He is not-white." In this second way, a certain improper mode of knowing and conceiving seems already to be intermixed. For since in the word "is" being itself is somehow included, something is already predicated in the manner of being which in fact is not being. And on this is founded or initiated another consideration of negation and privation insofar as they are beings of reason, about which consideration we will presently speak. But we must note that in these affirmations the manner in which the predicate is conceived is not attributed to the subject, such that [the predicate] is attributed in that manner to the subject. But there is attributed only that which is conceived, namely, the negation or the privation itself. Therefore, that affirmation is actually equivalent to a negation as far as it removes a predicate or insofar as through that copula there is affirmed only a truth of cognition, as Aristotle has indicated, in *Metaphysics*, Book 5, chapter 7.[160] Hence, when we say, for example, "Darkness is in the air," we are not signifying anything really inhering in the air, but only that the air lacks light and, therefore, can be truly known and said to be dark. All of this is common to both negation and privation considered in themselves.

---

155. For Soncinas, see note 151, above. For Nifo, see *Dilucidarium metaphysicarum disputationum*..., L. IV, disp. 2, pp. 107-109; cf. note 152, above.
156. Chrysostomi Iavelli Canapicii, *In omnibus Metaphysicae libris quaesita textualia metaphysicali modo determinata*, Lib. X, q. 10; ed. Venetiis, 1576, p. 276.
157. Cf. *In Ium Contra Gentiles*, c. 71; ed. Leonina, XIII (Romae, 1918), p. 208, n. 5. Here I am reading "chapter 71" from Salamanca 1597 (II, 722) and Mainz 1605 (II, 656), instead of "chapter 17" from the Vivès text.
158. Cf. *Defensiones*, II, d. 39, qu.1, art. 3, n. 1, ad 5 (ed. Paban-Pègues), II, p. 448.
159. See Aegidius Romanus, *Commentaria in libros Sententiarum*, I, dist. 36, q. 4 (*Utrum mala habeant ideam.*); ed. Venetiis (1521), 188v-189v, esp. 189r.
160. Cf. 1017a 32-34.

### How, As They Are Found in Reality, Negation and Privation Differ.

7. However, they differ, first, because privation means a lack of form in a naturally apt subject; but negation means a lack without any subjective aptitude. It is indeed necessary to add this, in order that it be distinguished from privation, or from the general notion of a lack, which can be common to both privation and negation. This diversity, however, is not in the proper and formal character which privation and negation directly express, but rather in what is connoted. For privation as such does not intrinsically include a subject or its aptitude. Otherwise, a privation would not be distinguished from a deprived subject, which is, as it were, a composite of subject and privation. And it would not be a purely unreal being, but it would consist of the reality of a potency and the negation of an act or a form – which contradicts the nature of a privation. Therefore, a privation formally entails only a negation, while restricting it to a subject with a capacity for the opposite form. In this way, it is said to differ from a negation obliquely and insofar as it connotes a subject with an aptitude for the opposite form. This kind of difference is customarily found also among positive forms conceived or signified in such a way. For in this way Aristotle often says "snubness" differs from "curvature."[161] For, although they formally express the same figure, nevertheless, "snubness" signifies it with respect to a certain kind of matter, which difference is not essential, but material. This, then, is the way we should think about negation and privation.

### The Division of Privations.

8. From this difference, we can infer a manifold distinction of privations, which Aristotle has touched upon in *Metaphysics*, Book 5, chapter 22.[162] For since privation entails a negation with a connotation of an aptitude, sometimes this aptitude is taken so improperly that it may be connoted not in the subject to which the privation is ascribed, but in beings absolutely. For example, if a plant (which is Aristotle's example) is said to be deprived of eyes. But sometimes that aptitude is connoted in a thing to which a privation is ascribed, not according to species but according to

---

161. Cf. *Metaphysics* VI, c. 1, 1025b 31-1026a 1; *ibid*. VII, c. 5, 1030b 28-1031a 1; and *ibid*., c. 11; 1037a 30-33,
162. Cf. 1022b 22-1023a 6.

genus only; for example, if a mole is said to be blind. Thirdly, an aptitude is connoted in a thing according to species, but not according to the time and all the circumstances required; for example, if an infant is said to be deprived of teeth. Fourthly, and more properly, an aptitude is connoted in a thing according to species and according to all circumstances which are required for such an aptitude. Moreover, privation sometimes connotes only an aptitude or a capacity, as darkness or night with respect[163] to air. But sometimes it connotes not only capacity, but also some principle by reason of which the opposite form should be present. Thus, for example, the resting of the earth around its center[164] or of the highest sphere of heaven in its place,[165] although it may be a privation of motion in the first way, is not such, however, in the second way. For no motion ought to be present in a body of this kind existing in such a place. But the lack of cold or dryness with respect to earth would be the privation of a perfection which ought to be present, which, most of all, is a proper privation. In this way, it is usual to distinguish a certain "ignorance of negation" and another "of privation."[166] For, although both presuppose capacity and, on this score, both have the character of privation, nonetheless, that which is a lack of knowledge that should be present has a more proper and rigorous character of privation, so that by comparison with it the other is deemed a negation. Since, therefore, privation and negation adequately divide [the notion of] lack, in as many ways as privation is multiplied, so negation can be multiplied in just as many ways. For, as much as we recede from one, so much do we approach the other, and vice versa.

9. Again, from Aristotle as cited above,[167] privation is distinguished into total privation or privation only in part. For example, something is said to be invisible [1] which lacks color, or [2] which has it very faded (*valde remissum*), and so with other things. Of these, the first is absolutely a privation in reality as well as in our way of speaking. The second, however, although it may be the custom sometimes in our way of speaking to signify it in the manner of an absolute privation, is actually a privation only compared to what it negates. For if it leaves some remainder [*si quid*

---

163. Here I am reading *respectu* from Salamanca, 1597 (II, 722) and Mainz, 1605 (II, 656), rather than *respectus* from the Vivès edition.
164. Cf. Aristotle, *De Coelo* II, c. 14, 296b 23-24.
165. For Aristotle the outermost sphere rests in its place because there is no place outside it to which it might move; cf. *De Coelo* I, c. 9, 279a 18-19; also cf. *Physics* IV, c. 4, 212a 18-24. For Suárez, while such movement would not be natural, it could be possible by the "absolute power" of God; cf. *DM* 51, 1, n. 21 (XXVI, 978).
166. That is, negative vs. privative ignorance
167. See paragraph n. 8, immediately preceding.

*relinquit*], with regard to that it is not truly a privation, as is self evident.

## An Incidental Doubt is Resolved: Whether a Privation May Be Subject to More and Less.

10. In consequence, this question is incidentally and easily answered: whether a privation is subject to more and less? For a distinction is also usually made between a negation and a privation insofar as a negation is not subject to more and less, but a privation is so subject. If, however, we speak of these with proportion, there is almost no difference in this. For, if a privation is total, there cannot be another formally and in itself greater than that. Another privation, however, could be less, if it is not total, but only partial. In the same way, among partial privations themselves there could be a greater and a less, by reason of the form to which they are opposed. For, if a form has degrees of intension, that will be physically a greater privation which will remove more degrees of the form from the subject. Indeed, that will be greatest which entirely removes the form. Perhaps, however, there could not be any least. For there is no smallest part of a form which could be taken away by remission.[168] But if the opposite form has a range of extension, the privation also could be extensively greater or less with the same proportion, and as considered physically. I always add this, because the weight or the quantity of a privation can be measured morally [i.e., in a moral context] from another angle, namely, from greater [or lesser] obligation of possessing such a form. Also, in the genus of imperfection or of evil, there will simply be greater imperfection or privation if the opposite form is more obligatory, even if otherwise the negation is equal. I have also said that total privation in itself and formally cannot be greater, for sometimes, from the side of its cause or its foundation, one privation is said to be greater than another. For example, a blindness, which has a much stronger (*vehementiorem*) cause, is called greater, even if it does not take away more of the form [of sight]. In this way also, one immateriality is said to be greater than another, and the same is true of other things. However, as is clear from the explanation itself, all this inequality invariably results from a positive reality, which either causes or grounds the privation, or really [is operative] at least inasmuch as it is not removed by that [privation] but is left in the subject. Almost all of this can with proportion be applied to

---

168. That is to say, on one side a limit will be reached with a complete removal, whereas on the other side there can be no limit for a smallest removal.

negation. For a negation can also be understood to be either total or partial, and a negation may have a greater or a lesser cause.

11. *A Negation can be necessary for a subject, but not a privation.* – There does seem to be one difference in this between a privation and a negation. For a negation, because it does not presuppose aptitude in a subject, can be necessary and its opposite affirmation impossible. In this it can be said to have the precise quasi-essence of a negation. But a privation, if it is most proper, can never be necessary with respect to its appropriate subject, for it presupposes potency to the opposite act. Where, however, there is a potency to contraries, neither extreme is absolutely impossible or necessary, according to the doctrine of Aristotle, in *Metaphysics*, Book IX.[169] From which difference another can be inferred: a negation can have an intrinsic and quasi-essential positive foundation in the subject to which it is attributed; but a proper privation, since it belongs accidentally, comes from outside the subject and from a quasi-extrinsic foundation, as has been suggested above[170] in explaining some of the agreement between privation and negation.

12. *The Difference Between a Privation [and a Negation] etc.* – *Whether things negatively opposed lack something in between, whereas things privatively opposed have something in between.* – Moreover, from what has been said we can infer another difference which is usually noted between privation and negation. Between a negation and an opposite affirmation there is no medium; but between privation and possession (*habitum*) there is a medium. We should note concerning this difference that in it we are not speaking of affirmation and negation as they are found in the mind's composing and dividing. For in this way, in a case of genuine contradiction, there is never something between an affirmation and a negation, whether what is affirmed and denied is something positive or something privative. For, just as it is necessary either that something see or not see, so it is also necessary either that it be blind or not be blind – as long as the affirmation and the negation concern the exact same subject and have the same signification or meaning of the predicate. But if there is not a perfect contradiction, but either contrariety or subcontrariety, then in each instance there can be something in between. As is clear from logic, this may be either through removal from or through partaking in either extreme.[171] Hence, we are not talking here about those

---

169. Cf. *Metaphysics* IX, c. 9; 1051a 4ff.
170. Cf. this Section, n. 4.
171. Just as, for example, an in-between gray can be more or less black or white, something between contrary or sub-contrary propositions can be nearer to one or the other opposite extreme.

judgments of the mind, but about a simple privation or negation, as compared with the opposite form which they remove. We express such through these terms, "blind," "not-seeing," and the like. And, in this way, a difference is established with respect to the same subject.

13. This can be explained through two affirmations, in which predicates, either contradictorily or privatively opposed, are predicated of the same subject. For those which are contradictorily opposed do not have anything in between. But of any subject at all one of them is truly said, and it is impossible that both be simultaneously affirmed or denied without one proposition being true and the other being false. In this way, Aristotle everywhere teaches that there is nothing in between contradictories; cf. *Metaphysics*, Book X, chapters 6 [sic][172] and 10,[173] and *Posterior Analytics*, Book I, chapter 2.[174] The reason is that nothing can be envisioned in between being and non-being. *You may say*: "Becoming" (*fieri*) is in between. *I answer*: it is a something in between perfect being and complete non-being, but not, however, absolutely between being and non-being. For absolutely it is something, and consequently in some way being, as is taken from Aristotle, *Metaphysics*, Book IV, chapter 2.[175] From this, the reasoning is better explained. For a negation simply removes a form, i.e., that which it negates, and it requires no special condition in the subject. Therefore, it is necessary that either the form or the negation of the form belong in the subject. However, in things privatively opposed there is something in between, not indeed through the participation of either extreme,[176] but through a removal, because privation does not mean negation without qualification, but negation with the connotation of aptitude in a subject. Therefore, from the lack of this connoted feature a subject can exist, to which neither of the opposites belongs. For example, a stone is not blind and it does not see, and yet it is necessarily either seeing or non-seeing. From this it is further understood that, in the case of a proper subject having an aptitude for a form, there cannot be a medium between privative opposites. For such opposites virtually include a contradictory opposition. Therefore, although the aforesaid difference is true as explained, nevertheless, there is inferred from it a proportional agreement. For, just as between something positive and its negation there is no medium with respect to any subject whatever, since for a negation or

---

172. Cf. *Metaphysics* X, c. 7; 1057a 34-35.
173. Cf. 1059a 6ff.
174. Cf. 72a 13.
175. Cf.1003b 10-11.
176. Cf. note 171, above.

an opposite affirmation any thing at all can be an apt subject, so also for a proportionate subject there exists no medium between something positive and its privation.

14. But *an objection occurs*: for even between contradictorily opposite terms there is a medium "by denial" (*per abnegationem*), at least with respect to a non-existing subject. For example, a chimera is neither white, nor is it not-white, because each affirmation is false inasmuch as it concerns "a non-supposing subject" (*de subjecto non supponente*).[177] A first answer is that a negation does not have something in between, if it is taken in the sense of a pure negation. But if something positive is mixed with it, on that account it could have something in between. For example, if this is false, "A chimera is not-seeing" (*Chymaera est non videns*),[178] it is so not simply because sight is denied, but also because some entity or being is affirmed. Thus, in order that contradictorily opposed predicates never have anything between them, even when they are expressed by way of affirmation, it is necessary that they be taken with respect to a proper subject, which is some existing thing. And in this way some proportion is preserved between a negation and a privation. A second answer arises by denying what is assumed. For of these two propositions, the one which has a negative predicate is true, even if the subject does not exist, especially if (as the logicians say) that negation is taken not "infinitely" (*infinitanter*) but "negatively" (*neganter*).[179] This is necessary in order that the opposition be purely negative. Otherwise, some affirmation will be partly included, as was correctly said in the first answer, which then seems valid when the negation in question is taken infinitely.

15. *Privation is found only in true beings; negation is found also in fictions.* – Hence, another difference also can be inferred between a privation and a pure negation, inasmuch as a privation can be attributed only to true and real beings. For since a privation means a lack of form in a naturally apt subject, it can be attributed only to a true and real being, because an aptitude for a form exists only in a real being. To be sure, it can be attributed only to an existing thing, for since it presupposes an aptitude for form, it does not belong to a subject necessarily but rather contingently, as we were saying above[180] (for we are speaking of privation

---

177. On this, cf. above: *Introduction*, note 91.
178. It should be noted that in Suárez's Latin there is no hyphen. This will make it easier for him to move in what follows from a negation placed on an infinite term, "is non-seeing," to a simple negation of the copula, "is not seeing."
179. Cf. above: *Introduction*, note 93.
180. See n. 11, this *Section*.

taken properly and with rigor). But accidental and contingent predicates do not belong to things, nor can they be truly attributed to them, unless they are actually existing things. This, indeed, is true with regard to propositions of inherence (*de inesse*); for a non-existing man cannot truly be said to be blind. But it will be otherwise, if the proposition be modal or possible (*de possibili*); for it is truly said that [a non-existing man] can be blind. But in this latter case, it is not a privation that is attributed to that man, but rather a capacity for a privation, which is something positive and intrinsic.

16. A negation, however, can be attributed not only to true and existing beings, but also to fictitious and non-existing beings – not only by dividing, but also by composing and affirming. For this proposition, said with rigor, is true: "A chimera is a non-being," since, if it is a fictitious being, it is therefore a non-being. Hence, Aristotle, in *Metaphysics*, Book IV, chapter 2,[181] says this statement is true: "A non-being is a non-being, or nothing." But if it is a non-being, it is also a non-man, a non-horse, and any other similar thing contained under non-being. The reason for this, however, can be that even though these propositions have an affirmative form, nevertheless, in sense and signification they are equivalent to negations. Thus, although in the order of the sentence the negation is placed after the copula, nevertheless in its power and sense it falls upon it. Or in another way, the copula can be said to be independent of time. For in that way in which the subject is conceived as a fictitious being, the predicate is intrinsic to the nature of the subject, and thus that proposition can be not only true, but also necessary. And this answer, as well as the difference so explained, is not displeasing to me. I note only that what was said about privations must be understood about true and real privations. For there can also be some imaginary and contrived privations in fictitious beings, for example, if someone fancies a blind chimera, or conceives an imaginary space as dark, or something similar. Indeed, a privation of this kind could be attributed to a fictitious being in relation to a copula restricting (*abstrahentem*) or amplifying (*ampliantem*) that fictitious being.[182] In the

---

181. Cf. 1003b 10-11.
182. In this last sentence, Suárez is evidently stretching "ampliation" (the extension of the present copula to past or future) to imaginary time. This will be involved in his understanding of how such terms as "chimaera" will stand for (*supponere*) "things." Also, see above in this same paragraph, the independence of the copula from time and its extension to a fictitious being; cf. C. Berton, "Justification de la révision du texte des anciennes éditions et observations critiques," in Suárez, *Opera omnia*; Vol. 27, p. 390, at 1036, n. 16. In connection with this, also cf.: "Hence also the logicians say that imaginable being extends more broadly than possible being" (*Unde etiam dialectici dicunt ens imaginabile latius ampliare quam ens possibile.*); at Section 2, n. 18, above. On the doctrine of "ampliation" in the time of Suarez, cf. note 72, above; also see P. Fonseca, *Institutionum dialecticarum, Libri octo*. VIII, c. 37 (ed. Coimbra, 1964) II, pp. 726-728, who

same way, to certain fictitious beings one can attribute negations of others, and to one negation another negation. Thus a chimera is conceived not to be a goat-stag (*hircocervus*), and imaginary space not to be something successive.

17. *Why Privation, but not Negation, is numbered among the Principles of Natural Things.* – Another difference can be specified between privation and negation. Privation is numbered among the principles of real change or generation; but negation, as such, cannot take on the character of this kind of principle. The first part is known from Aristotle, in *Physics*, Book I,[183] and *Metaphysics*, Book XI,[184] where he places privation among the principles of a material thing. The second part, however, is proven inasmuch as a natural change cannot come to be from just any negation. The reason for both parts is that change can come about only in a subject which is capable [of undergoing change]. Thus, the lack, which is presupposed in it, must have the character of a privation, since it is a negation in a naturally apt subject. Therefore, that which would be a pure negation, and would not take on the character of a privation, could not be a principle of change. This, however, is not the place for us to explain how a privation may take on the character of a principle. That properly pertains to the first book of the *Physics*, and for the purpose of the present subject matter it was sufficiently touched upon above, in *Disputation* 12, section 1.[185] For it is not a properly influencing principle, but rather a directly necessary terminus from which the change comes to be. From this, however, there is rightly confirmed what, with Cajetan and others, we said above.[186] Looked at in itself, a privation, even though it is not a real being, is not something contrived by the reason. Rather, it is a kind of lack which in its own way is found in things themselves. For, apart from every fiction of the reason, natural change can have its own necessary principles, one of which is privation.

18. *You may say*: negation also, considered in itself, belongs to things without any intellectual fiction, i.e., "by removing" (*removendo*), as we also said above.[187] *The answer is* that negation cannot be a principle of

---

rejects ampliation in the instance of merely imaginable things. For some treatment of what is involved here, cf. V. Muñoz Delgado, *La Logica nominalista en la universidad de Salamanca (1510-1530)*, (Madrid, 1964), esp. pp. 238-243; and E. J. Ashworth, "Chimeras and Imaginary Objects: A Study in Post-Medieval Theory of Signification," *Vivarium*, XV (1977), esp. pp. 72-7.
183. Cf. *Physics* I, c. 8; 191b 15ff.
184. Cf. *Metaphysics* XI, c. 3; 1061a 18ff.
185. Cf. *DM* 12, s. 1 (XXV, pp. 373-383).
186. See *Section* III, n. 3.
187. Cf. *Section* V, n. 2.

natural change, not for the lack of this condition, but because of itself it does not require a subject capable of the opposite form, which is a requirement for natural change. Hence, it can be further said that, although negation alone could not be a sufficient principle of change, nevertheless, in its own genre, and in the character of a *terminus a quo*, some negation could be a sufficient principle of some action or production. In this way creation is called coming to be from nothing, just as generation [is called coming to be] from privation. But "nothing" here means a mere negation. It can be added, however, that the character of a principle is not attributed to nothing itself with respect to creation as properly as it is to privation with respect to generation. For privation, at least on the side of the subject, connotes or includes some positive reality, which seems necessary for the proper nature of a principle. But we have spoken about this elsewhere.[188]

**Whether there can be a Regress from Privation to Possession (*Habitum*).**

19. The thought just occurred that in this place we should explain that common axiom: *From privation to possession there is no regress*. This is taken from Aristotle, *De Generatione*, Book 2,[189] and *Metaphysics*, Book VIII, chapter 5,[190] where[191] [in comment] we briefly stated it to be true for a form which is numerically the same, but not for a form which is the same in species, except as regards an immediate regress, and that not in all forms, but in certain ones which by their nature determine a definite order among themselves. There, with Aristotle, we spoke about a form which can be induced through a proper action or generation, and about the privation opposite to it. But there are certain accidental forms which by natural necessity flow from some intrinsic principle and which cannot come to be otherwise. If a privation occurs in these, there cannot be a regress to a possession that is either numerically or specifically the same. Blindness or deafness seem to be of this kind, and on that account they cannot be naturally removed. For there is in nature no intrinsic principle which could restore the organ of a certain faculty to that disposition for

---

188. On the nature of a principle, as distinguished from a cause, see Suárez, *DM* 12, s. 1 (XXV, 373-383). For privation as a principle of natural generation, see *ibid.*, n. 6 (p. 374).
189. Cf. chapter 11; 338b 9ff.
190. Cf. 1045a 3ff.
191. Cf. Suárez, *DM*, *Index locupletissimus*, Bk. V, q. 2 (XXV, xlv-xlvi).

the want of which it lost even the faculty itself. But these matters are now going beyond the treatment of beings of reason, with which we are concerned in this Disputation. Therefore, let this suffice for the first consideration[192] of privation and negation.

**Privation and Negation are compared as they are Beings of Reason.**

20. *Privation has very great similarity with quality.* – We can treat of privation and negation in a second way, insofar as they are formally beings of reason.[193] In this way also, they agree in everything common to being of reason as such, or to (so to speak) "absolute" being of reason, i.e., as it is distinguished from the being of reason that is a relation – which is clear enough from what was said in sections above.[194] Hence, it seems common to each to be fashioned or thought as a sort of quality affecting the subject which it denominates, although not equally or in the same way. For with regard to privation that seems universally true. For example, blindness is apprehended as a certain disposition of a particular organ, and darkness as a disposition of air. Indeed, whatever we apprehend in the manner of a positive being must be conceived by analogy or proportion with a being of some real category.[195] However, the apprehension of a privation in relation to a thing which it denominates has a greater similarity with quality than with any other category.

21. *An Objection is Answered.* – You may say: that is true when the form to which the privation is opposed is a quality, but it is false if it is a thing of another category. *I answer* by denying what is assumed. I will show this by briefly running through the other categories.[196] For the privation of a substantial form is not apprehended in matter like a substantial form, but like an accidental disposition, which can be present or absent. Thus it also imitates a quality. Quantity, however, is not naturally separable [from a material substance], and therefore a privation of quantity is not naturally given. If, however, we posit a material substance deprived of quantity by the absolute power [of God],[197] we will not apprehend that

---

192. That is, insofar as they are in things themselves and "remove some form or positive entity"; cf. this *Section*, n. 1, above.
193. As opposed to the first way, i.e., insofar as they are in things; cf. this *Section*, nn. 2-19.
194. Cf. *Section* III, nn. 8 and 9; *Section* IV; n. 10.
195. With this compare C. Giacon, as cited in note 8, *Introduction*, above.
196. Note that the issue here is both similar to and different from that which principally occupied Suárez in *Section* IV, above. Here his concern is with categories of *negative* beings of reason; there it was with *positive* beings of reason.
197. On the absolute versus the ordinary power of God, cf. Suárez, *DM* 30, s. 17, nn. 32-36 (XXVI, 216-218). For discussion of the absolute and the ordained power of God up to Luther, see Richard P. Desharnais, *The History of the Distinction between God's Abso-*

privation as a quantity, but rather like a certain immaterial and simple disposition. And the reason for the difference between quantity and quality seems to be that a quantity [in things themselves] never has another quantity contrary to itself.[198] Therefore, the lack of a quantity is not apprehended as an opposite quantity, but as a certain disposition of another character, having a formal effect of a far different nature from the whole category of quantity. However, one quality can have another contrary to itself. Hence, it happens that, when a quality does not have a contrary, its privation can be apprehended in the manner of an opposite quality, and as having a formal effect opposite to the effect of the contrary quality, not however outside the scope or the range (*proportionem*) of the whole category of quality. By almost the same reasoning, I said above[199] that the privation of a *relation* is not, as such, conceived like a relation. For through such a privation, proportion and likeness to a true relation is destroyed, inasmuch as order to another is negated. I do not deny, however, that with the privation of one relation there could be understood another, positively opposite or diverse, sometimes real or sometimes of reason. For example, when someone is deprived of the relation of similitude there can arise a real relation of dissimilitude. And in one who is deprived of the relation of sonship by the death of a father, there can be conceived a relation of reason to a parent who has now passed away. However, this is not the conception of a privation as such, but of another form.[200]

22. The same can easily be understood in the remaining categories, insofar as some manner of privation can be found in them. For in *action*, as such, there does not seem properly to be any privation, because action does not relate to an agent as to a subject, but rather as to a principle.[201] With regard to an agent, therefore, a lack of action is not properly a negation in a naturally apt subject, and thus it is not properly a privation. But, whatever kind of negation or privation it may be, it is not conceived like

---

*lute and Ordained Power and Its Influence on Martin Luther*, unpublished Ph.D. dissertation, Catholic University of America: Washington, D.C., 1966; also cf. Mary Ann Pernoud, "The Theory of the *Potentia Dei* According to Aquinas, Scotus, and Ockham," *Antonianum* XLVII (1972), pp. 69-95, and W. J. Courtney, *Capacity and Volition. A History of the Distinction of Absolute and Ordained Power* (Bergamo, 1990).

198. For this, see Aristotle, *Categories*, c. 6, 5b 11 - 6a 18; and Suárez, *DM* 41, 5, n. 2 (XXVI, 600).
199. Cf. *Section* III, n. 7.
200. Compare what was said in *Section* III, n. 7, above, about being an orphan.
201. That action does not inhere in the agent as in a subject: *DM* 48, s. 4 (XXVI, pp. 888-893), esp. n. 15 (p. 892). That action relates to the agent as to a principle: *DM* 48, s. 1 (XXVI, 668-873); esp. n. 17 (p. 872).

an action, because it is not conceived as flowing from an agent. Similarly, although with regard to *passion* (and the same is true about change and motion) a privation may properly exist, still, this is not conceived in the manner of a passion. For it is not conceived as something becoming (*aliquid in fieri*), but as something already in existence and at rest (*in facto esse ac quieto*). In this way, rest, which is a privation of motion, is not apprehended as a passion, but as a quasi-disposition of a certain thing remaining at rest. In *duration*, certainly, there is never a proper and pure privation, because duration cannot be entirely taken away unless its subject is destroyed.[202] Neither, I think, is *place* (*ubi*) taken away through a pure privation, but through an opposite place; and the argument is the same for *position* (*situs*) in things which are capable of it. Therefore, privations which are beings of reason[203] are not fashioned in those categories. And if they are conceived in some way positively, it is only by conceiving some relations, such as absence or distance of place or time. Finally, as regards [the category of] *habit*, there is conceived [only] a sort of privation (*quaedam privatio*). For a man is not properly the subject of a garment; and in the way that he can have a character of privation, it is not conceived like a habit. For it is not conceived in the manner of something contiguous, but rather as something quasi-inherent. Neither is its effect conceived as analogous to the effect of a habit, but rather as completely outside the whole range of habit. Therefore, it seems correctly said that true and proper privation is universally apprehended and thought in the manner of a quality.

23. *What True Category of Being Does Negation Resemble?* – In the case of negation, however, that general rule does not appear universally true, but there is need for distinction. For in one way, a negation is conceived as a disposition of some subject which lacks a certain nature or form. In this case, the reasoning about negation seems almost the same as that about privation, and everything which was said [about privation] can be easily applied [to negation]. In addition, however, negation is such that it could be apprehended apart from any subject. But this is not possible for a privation since it intrinsically means negation in a naturally apt subject. Moreover, a simple negation is apprehended not just in the manner of a quality, but also after the pattern of other categories. For we said

---

202. That duration cannot be entirely taken away unless its subject is destroyed seems clear inasmuch as duration is nothing else than the permanence of something in being; on this, see Suárez, *DM* 50, s. 1 (XXV, 912-916); esp. *ibid.*, n. 7 (p. 915).
203. To understand Suárez through paragraphs 21 and 22, one's focus must be kept on privation as a being of reason, rather than on privation as existing in things themselves.

above[204] that impossible beings, fashioned in the manner of substances, are included under negation. Likewise, imaginary space, which we conceive as having dimensions, is not in fact a proper privation, but a kind of negation. For no subject or real capacity is presupposed for it. Therefore, it also belongs under negation. And the same is true about time or imaginary succession, which is pictured outside all subjects.

24. *A Privation is always conceived as existing in Something; A Negation is conceived otherwise.* – From this, we may gather a further difference between negation and privation. As has been explained,[205] a privation is always conceived as something adhering to or joined to some subject. But a negation is not always so conceived. For *nothing* itself is a certain negation which is not understood to adhere to anything. And the same is evident from the other examples adduced above.[206]

25. *How great is the diversity between Negation and Privation?* – Hence also, we can conjecture, when, according to the way of our conceiving (*nostro concipiendi modo*),[207] the diversity between these two members is essential, or when it is only accidental or material. For a negation which is conceived as it were directly, and of its nature outside a subject, is formally different from a privation, and consequently also from that sort of negation which is conceived as of itself adhering to something and denominating that thing.[208] This is because they are apprehended under different notions of being, such as being in the manner of something existing through itself or in itself versus being as something existing in another.[209] Privation, however, and that negation which is conceived as something existing in another, need not differ essentially, but rather by the difference of the forms to which they are opposed. In this way also, negations are distinguished among themselves and privations among themselves, as St. Thomas has remarked, in *Summa Theologiae*, I-II, q. 71, a. 6 [sic], ad 1.[210] Although, indeed, this is principally true about negations and privations taken fundamentally,[211] nevertheless, from that it is

---

204. Cf. *Section* IV, n. 10.
205. Cf. n. 7, this *Section*.
206. Cf. paragraph 23, immediately preceding.
207. Literally: "according to our way of conceiving." My translation tries to avoid any suggestion of subjectivism or even hesitation by Suárez and to highlight the fact that he continues to be focused on negation and privation as beings in the mind's conception rather than in things themselves.
208. Contrast a pure negation with the negation in a man of a faculty for neighing; cf. this *Section*, n. 4, above.
209. That is, being in the manner of substance versus being in the manner of accident.
210. For this, see *Summa Theologiae* I-II, q. 72, a. 9, ad 1; ed. Leonina, VII (1892), p. 23.
211. That is, as they are found in things themselves.

also formally true of these insofar as they are beings of reason. For blindness and deafness, insofar as they are apprehended in the manner of beings, are also apprehended as diverse. The same is true proportionately in the case of negations compared among themselves. Hence, even more so, if a privation and a negation are opposed to forms essentially diverse, they also in their own order will have a similar or proportional diversity – not because they are a privation and a negation, but because they are such with respect to those forms.

26. But when a privation and a negation are of the same form in comparison with diverse subjects, as, for example, the negation of sight with respect to a man and to an angel, then they do not indeed seem to differ essentially in the character of "being of reason," but only by a denomination or a relation taken from an order to the diverse subjects. This is clear, because in real and positive forms a comparison to diverse subjects does not cause an essential difference in the form, but only different denominations or relations, as long as the entity of the form, considered in itself, otherwise has the same constitutive principle.[212] For example, whiteness in snow or whiteness in a crow will be of the same species, even though in the one it is a connatural property while, if it were in the other, it would be abnormal (*violenta*) and preternatural. Again, the same motion downward is natural to earth and violent to air, but it is not on that account specifically different in being. In a similar way, therefore, the lack of sight [in either a man or an angel] is in itself of the same nature, because it always has the same specifying principle and it is apprehended under the same character of being. But with respect to an angel, on account of that angel's incapacity, a lack of sight has only the character of a negation, while with respect to a man it is called a privation. Following from this, the two instances also differ under the aspect of evil, inasmuch as that lack is an evil for a man, but not for an angel. Likewise, it can be termed unnatural (*violenta*) for a man, but connatural[213] for an angel. However, this must be understood about that lack as considered in itself. For if we are speaking of it "in composite sense" (*in sensu composito*),[214]

---

212. That is to say, the same basic formal causality. Cf. his equivalent phrase, "the same specifying principle," immediately below.
213. "Connatural" here is slightly different from "natural". Whereas, "natural" is used to designate something which stems directly and commensurably from some nature (e.g. a property), "connatural" designates something which accompanies some nature without directly stemming from it.
214. Suárez's meaning here is plain. A "lack," as such, would be understood simply, or as the Scholastics would say, "in divided sense" (*in sensu diviso*). But "a lack which is a negation" or "a lack which is a privation," i.e., a lack with an added specification, is a lack "in composite sense" (*in sensu composito*). On *sensus compositus* and *sensus divisus*, see Fonseca, *Institutionum* . . . , VIII, cc. 6 and 7; ed. Ferreira Gomes, pp. 636-646.

i.e., designated as a privation or a pure negation, in these ways it includes diverse relations of reason to diverse subjects, which relations are essential to the designated forms,[215] [precisely] as they are under such designations.

27. Finally, as I was saying above,[216] we are speaking here about negation as it is conceived in the manner of a simple (*incomplexae*) form. For if we speak of complex negations, then we can understand an essential diversity between lacks, in relation to diverse subjects with which they are compared as negation or privation. For this negation, "An angel does not have sight," or this affirmation, "An angel is non-seeing," are very different from these: "A man is blind" or "[A man] lacks sight" (*Homo est caecus, aut caret visu*).[217] For the former are necessary propositions, whereas the latter are contingent. Hence, they have an essential diversity. That is not strange, because with respect to a proposition (*complexionis*) the terms (*extrema*) themselves are compared as composing it. Therefore, when one or other term is varied, the composition and the condition (*habitudo*) of the proposition is varied. But the fact is otherwise for a simple form taken by itself. For it intrinsically includes not this or that subject, but a disposition to, as it were, an appropriate subject.

## Section VI.
## What is Necessary for a Relation of Reason, And in How Many Ways may it be Fashioned or Contrived?

1. *A Description of Relation of Reason.* – Since a relation of reason is distinguished from all absolute things through the common, or quasi-common, character of relation, but from real relations by the fact that it is not a true and real relation, in general it can be defined by negation of a real relation, so that a relation of reason is every relation which is not real. But because, apart from some fiction or conception of the intellect, that negation cannot be understood as combined with what relation says in a positive way, therefore, a relation of reason can be generally defined

---

215. "Forms" here is used metaphorically to refer to privations or pure negations. On this, cf. the immediately following sentence in paragraph 27.
216. See this Section, n. 12; also, Section II, n. 15.
217. Literally: "A man is blind or lacks sight." I believe Suárez's language here complicates (if not negates) the point he is making. He is speaking of negative judgments or propositions. But his expressions are not negative propositions, except equivalently ("by way of affirmation"?).

in a positive manner as a relation which the intellect fashions like a form ordered to something else, or a form relating one thing, which in fact is not ordered or related, to some other thing.

### What is Necessary for a Relation of Reason?

2. Therefore, since a relation of reason lacks the truth of a real relation, and is a kind of shadow of that, it seems to require two things. One is, that it not have all the features usually needed for a real relation, i.e., a capable subject, a real foundation with a proper (*debita*) "founding reason" (*ratione fundandi*),[218] and a real terminus actually existing with a sufficient real, or in the nature of things (*ex natura rei*), foundation – about which much has been said above.[219] Thus, all these features, taken together, cannot be the same (*communia*) for a relation of reason. Otherwise, this relation could in no way be distinguished from a real relation. The second requirement is, that something of these features which concur for a real relation in some, at least remote, way should provide a foundation for a relation of reason. Or rather, it should provide a foundation for the thinking and the manner of conceiving, by which a relation of reason is fabricated, with the intellect itself providing what is lacking in reality for a true relation. I say, however, there is need of something in reality which at least remotely provides a foundation or gives an occasion for this relation. For, as I have repeatedly said,[220] we are treating of beings of reason which in some way contribute to the knowledge of real beings, and which always have some foundation in reality. But if we want completely to encompass relations of reason, we can add that a relation of reason is that which lacks some condition necessary for a real relation, or which lacks all conditions, but for which something analogous to these is fashioned or thought by the intellect.

### A First Division of Relation of Reason.

3. Therefore, the first division of relation of reason can be said to be into that which is completely fabricated by the intellect, without any foundation in reality, and that which has some, but not enough, foundation in reality. By the word "foundation," I am now understanding all the

---

218. For Suárez on the foundation *vis à vis* the "reason for founding" for a relation, cf. *DM* 47, s. 7, nn. 10-14 (XXVI, 813-814).
219. See Suárez, *DM* 47, ss. 6-9 (XXVI, 808-820).
220. See above: *Prologue*, n. 1; *Section* I, n. 2; *Section* IV, n. 2; and *Section* IV, n. 10.

conditions necessary for a real relation. In the first member of the division are contained all relations of reason which are thought among other beings of reason, especially if such beings of reason are simply fictitious. An example is the relation of similarity between two chimerae, or the relation of dissimilarity between a chimera and a goat-stag, and the like. Also to this member can belong relations of reason between two privations. In this way, one dark place is said to be similar to another, and in imaginary space there is conceived a relation of distance, and in imaginary succession a relation of prior and posterior. However, these relations, founded on the privations and the negations of things, have some greater, at least remote, foundation in those things.[221] Thirdly, to this member can be reduced relations of reason among real possible, but not existing, beings. For example, take the relation of antecedence of Adam to the Antichrist, and similar relations. These have a greater foundation in things inasmuch as their extremes are not entirely beings of reason, although as they are apprehended as extremes or subjects of relations they are beings of reason. Hence, in these three orders of relations, which we are numbering under that first member, there is contained a kind of sub-division of that member. And under these orders, almost all manner of real [sic] relations can be easily thought by a certain analogy or proportion.

**The Second Division of Relations.**

4. But relations of reason which have some foundation in existing things can be further sub-divided, on the basis of their different foundations, or, conversely, from their various lacks of those conditions required for a real relation. Hence, first under this member, those relations can be placed which are attributed to an existing thing with regard to a non-existing terminus, whether this last be a possible being or a fictitious being. For example, take a relation of priority of an existing Peter to a future Antichrist, or a relation of diversity of an existing Peter to a chimera. For equal reason, there belongs to this order a corresponding relation of reason in the other extreme, of non-being to being,[222] or of a being of reason to a real being.[223] For in these there is lacking a necessary condition for a real relation on the part of one term (*ex parte termini*),

---

221. That is, they have a greater foundation than do relations among simply fictitious things.
222. That is, a relation of posteriority of the Antichrist to Peter.
223. That is, a relation of diversity of the chimaera to Peter.

namely, that it be real and really existing. Also in this order, we can subdivide those three modes of relations (*relativorum*) which are founded in unity, in action, or in the character of measure.[224] For all these are relations of reason, when one or other extreme is not real and existing.

5. In second place under this member are relations that are conceived between extremes which are something real, but which do not in fact have a real distinction or one that is actual from the nature of things (*ex natura rei*), but one of reason only. For there is lacking here another condition required for a real relation. And following upon different distinctions of reason between the extremes of this relation, there will be diversity also among relations of this kind. For sometimes there is only a purely rational (*rationis ratiocinantis*) distinction, as in a relation of identity of the same thing with itself. But sometimes there is a grounded rational distinction (*rationis ratiocinatae*),[225] which is fundamental or virtual in reality – as in the relation of distinction among the divine attributes, and similarly in other cases. But in relations of this kind, with the mentioned lack of distinction in a thing itself (*in re ipsa*), there is supposed some foundation of unity or distinction in effects, or acts, or the like, from which the intellect may take occasion to fashion similar relations, as is easily evident from the proposed examples. Hence, to this class of relation of reason one can also reduce those which, although they are employed among distinct things, are employed, however, without enough distinction of the foundation, because, to be sure, it is one and the same in both extremes. For example, take the relation of similarity or equality among the divine persons, about which we have spoken above.[226]

6. Placed third in this order are those relations of reason which, although they are employed among things distinct and otherwise capable of real categorical relations, are however rational (*rationis*) from the lack of an intrinsic foundation, either in both or in one extreme (which can amount to two members of this class). Hence, first, all relations belong to this class which are founded in both extremes only upon an extrinsic denomination. Take, for example, the relation of a stipulated (*ad placitum*) sign, which both in the sign and in the significate is a relation of reason, whether such a sign is a word, such as a noun or a verb, or whether it is a thing, such as a sacrament. For since this imposition in order to

---

224. For this, see Aristotle, *Metaphysics* V, c. 15; 1020b 26-31. Also see Suárez, *DM* 47, ss. 10-15 (XXVI, 820-847).
225. On the difference between a *distinctio rationis ratiocinantis* and a *distinctio rationis ratiocinatae*, cf. Suárez, *DM* 7, s. 1, n. 4 (XXV, 251).
226. Cf *DM* 47, s. 11, n. 13 (XXVI, 829).

signify does not posit in the sign, or in the significate, any reality except an extrinsic denomination, it cannot, as all teach, be the foundation of a real relation. Of the same sort, moreover, are the relations among men of master and slave (*domini et servi*). For these are founded only upon a certain extrinsic denomination taken from the will. Many others are similar, for example, all those which arise from contracts and human wills, such as between husband and wife in the character of being spouses, between a seller and a buyer from their will to make a contract, and so with others.

7. In turn, to the second branch of this class belong all non-mutual relations, insofar as they are a matter of reason in one extreme. For example, take the relation of seen to one seeing, or of visible to vision, or of knowable to knowledge, etc., about which enough was said in *Disputation* 47.[227] Also to this section can be reduced all relations of God to existing creatures. For these too can be said to be founded on an extrinsic denomination, because in God Himself, considered as such (*secundum se*), there is no capacity, much less any foundation, for such relations.

8. Fourth and last, we can propose another member, made up of those relations, in which many of the aforesaid defects of features necessary for a real relation run together, with some remote foundation from the side of reality (*ex parte rei*) and a proximate foundation in some extrinsic denomination. Of this kind seem to be the relations of reason which are called "logical intentions," for example, relations of genus, species, predicate, subject, and the like. These relations, indeed, are sometimes ascribed to words, since predications and definitions are accomplished through the medium of words. But sometimes they are ascribed to things, because it is these which are known, subjected, and predicated – objectively.[228] And these are properly called logical intentions. For the former [i.e. those ascribed to words] either belong more to grammar or rhetoric, or are secondarily ascribed to words as to the instruments by which we manifest concepts and speak about things. Therefore, although in these relations the extremes are sometimes real, nevertheless, there is often a lack of sufficient distinction, for example, between animal and rational insofar as they are compared as genus and difference. Sometimes, also, there is not enough unity and existence in one or other extreme as so related. This happens in the case of a universal object as such with respect to singulars. For insofar as it is universal it does not exist, nor does it have

---

227. Cf. *DM* 47, s. 13 (XXVI, 835-837).
228. Suárez's point here is that things are known, and are subjects and predicates in propositions, through the medium of objective concepts. For example, see *DM* 8, 3, n. 17 (XXV, 288).

such [universal] unity in reality. Lastly, there is never in things themselves a sufficient foundation for relations of this kind. For these are founded on some extrinsic denomination from an act of the intellect.

**About Second Intentions.**

9. *Three Relations of Reason follow upon the three operations of the intellect.* – Therefore, following the three operations of the intellect there is also a threefold order of such relations. From the first operation there arise relations of genus, species, definition, defined, etc; from the second operation, the relation of predicate, subject, copula, proposition; and from the third, the relation of antecedent, consequent, middle, extremity, etc. For these relations belong to things not in themselves but as denominated from some operation of the intellect. Accordingly, they are always relations of reason, and not real, even though they may be employed at times among existing and distinct things. These relations, however, are fabricated not gratuitously, but with some foundation taken from reality. Such is either a real agreement, on which the abstraction of a universal is founded, which is modified also into a genus, a species, etc., insofar as the agreement is more or less. Or it is a real identity or a union of one thing with another, on which is based the affirmation of the one of the other. Or it is a real emanation of one thing from another, or a concomitance, or something similar, on which is based an *a priori* or an *a posteriori* inference.

10. *Why Relations of Genus, Species, and the like, should have claimed the name of "Second Intention."* – For this cause, these last relations of reason are usually called second intentions in a special way, as if resulting from a second intention, or attention, or consideration, of the intellect. By this name there is properly denoted a reflexive intellection, since it presupposes another with regard to which it is employed. Indeed, although, as we mentioned above,[229] all beings of reason can be said to be based in some way on the intellect's operation from which they arise, which operation always presupposes another concept of a real being after the pattern of which or on the occasion of which the being of reason is conceived, properly, however, that operation is reflex, and is (may I say so) essentially "second," which falls upon another cognition, or upon an object as it is denominated from a prior cognition and is receiving some properties from that fact. Therefore, because these logical relations are

---

229. Cf. *Section* II, n. 16

always based on reflex cognition of this kind, they are thus is a special way called "second intentions," or "second objective conceptions" (*secundae notiones objectivae*), because they are objects for a second conception or formal intention. Hence, by *antonomasia*,[230] these relations of reason are usually called things of second intention, not because every thing known through a reflex intellection is a being of reason (for it is evident that real intellection itself can be reflexly known), but because they have[231] their being only objectively in a second or reflex intellectual cognition.

11. From this it further stems that the intellect could again reflect upon those same second intentions, and consider the agreements or differences among them, and define them, or reason discursively from them, and thus base similar relations on them. In this way, from genus and species it abstracts the relation of universal, and denominates that a [new] genus, and the same is true in other cases. Therefore, these are relations of reason now not only on account of the other lacks [i.e. of the conditions of real relations], but because they are not employed proximately among real or existing things. Thus, when these relations are said to be in some way based on things, this must be understood about the first relations of this series (*ordinis*). But to say more about these relations belongs to the particular sciences, for these relations can be multiplied almost to infinity by fictions or reflexions of the intellect. Therefore, both about these and about this whole doctrine, let what we have said suffice and let it proceed in praise of a glorious God.

---

230. A figure of speech in which a name appropriate to different things is applied to one of them for which it is especially suited.
231. Here I read *habent* from Salamanca, 1597 (II, 728) and Mainz, 1605 (II, 661) instead of *habet* from the Vivès edition.

# Bibliography

## General Bibliographies

Iturrioz, J. "Bibliografía suareciana," *Pensamiento* 4, número extraordinario (1948), 603ff.

Solana, M. *Historia de la filosofía española, epoca del Renacimiento.* Madrid, 1941. III, 455ff.

Santos-Escudero, C. "Bibliografía suareciana de 1948 a 1980," *Cuadernos Salmantinos de Filosofía* 7 (1980), 337-75.

## Principal Latin Edition Used in this Work

Suarez, Franciscus, S.J. *Opera Omnia.* 26 vols. Paris: L. Vivès, 1856-1866; plus two volumes of indices, 1878.

## English Translations of Suárez

Suárez, Francisco. *Disputatio V: Individual Unity and its Principle.* Tr. Jorge J. E. Gracia, in *Suárez on Individuation.* Milwaukee: Marquette University Press, 1982.

──────. *On Formal and Universal Unity (Disputatio VI).* Tr. James F. Ross. Milwaukee: Marquette University Press, 1964.

──────. *On the Various Kinds of Distinctions (Disputatio VII).* Tr. Cyril Vollert. Milwaukee: Marquette University Press, 1947.

──────. *The Metaphysics of Good and Evil according to Suárez: Metaphysical Disputations X and XI and Selected Passages from Disputation XXII and Other Works.* Translation with Introduction, Notes, and Glossary, by Jorge J. E. Gracia and Douglas Davis. München: Philosophia Verlag, 1989.

──────. *On the Essence of Finite Being as Such, on the Existence of that Essence and their Distinction (Disputatio XXXI).* Translated from the Latin with an Introduction by Norman J. Wells. Milwaukee: Marquette University Press, 1983.

## Secondary Sources

Alejandro, J. M. *La gnoseología del Doctor Eximio y la acusación nominalista*. Comillas, 1948.

Burns, J. Patout. "Action in Suarez," *The New Scholasticism* 38 (1964), 453-472.

Conze, Eberhard. *Der Begriff der Metaphysik bei Franciscus Suarez*. Leipzig, 1928.

Copleston, Frederick, S.J.. *A History of Philosophy. Vol. 3: Ockham to Suarez*. Westminster, MD, 1953.

Courtine, Jean-François. *Suarez et le système de la métaphysique*. Paris, 1990.

Cronin, Timothy, S.J. *Objective Being in Descartes and in Suarez*. Rome: Gregorian University Press, 1966.

──────. "Eternal Truths in the Thought of Suarez and Descartes," *The Modern Schoolman* 38 (1961), 269-288.

Cruz, Miguel. "La intentionalidad en la filosofía de Franscisco Suárez," in *Congreso Internacional de Filosofía, Barcelona, 4-10 Octubre, 1948, Actas*. Madrid, 1949. I, 315-337.

Doig, James C., "Suarez, Descartes, and the Objective Reality of Ideas," *The New Scholasticism* 51 (1977), 350-371.

Doyle, John P., *The Metaphysical Nature of the Proof for God's Existence according to Francis Suarez, S.J.*. Unpublished Ph.D. dissertation, University of Toronto, 1966.

──────. "Suarez on the Reality of the Possibles," *The Modern Schoolman* 44 (1967), 29-40.

──────. "Suarez on the Analogy of Being," *The Modern Schoolman* 46 (1969), 219-249 and 323-341.

──────. "Heidegger and Scholastic Metaphysics," *The Modern Schoolman* 49 (1972), 201-220.

──────. "The Suarezian Proof for God's Existence," in *History of Philosophy in the Making: A Symposium of Essays to Honor Professor James D. Collins on his 65th Birthday*. Ed. Linus J. Thro. Washington, D.C., 1982. Pp. 105-117.

———. "The Conimbricenses on the Relations Involved in Signs," *Semiotics 1984*. New York, 1985. Pp. 567-576.

———. "*Prolegomena* to a Study of Extrinsic Denomination in the Work of Francis Suarez, S.J.," *Vivarium* XXII, 2 (1984), 121-160.

———. "Suarez on Truth and Mind-Dependent Beings: Implications for a Unified Semiotic," in *Semiotics 1983*. New York, 1987. Pp. 121-133.

———. "Suarez on Beings of Reason and Truth (1)," *Vivarium* 25 (1987), 47-75.

———. "Suarez on Beings of Reason and Truth (2)," *Vivarium* 26 (1988), 51-72.

———. "'Extrinsic Cognoscibility': A Seventeenth Century Supertranscendental Notion," *The Modern Schoolman* 68 (1990), 57-80.

———. "Suarez on the Unity of a Scientific Habit," *The American Catholic Philosophical Quarterly* 65 (1991), 309-331.

Drouin, Paul, M.S.C. "L'entitatif et l'intentionnel: étude comparée de la doctrine thomiste et de l'enseignement suarezian," *Laval théologique et philosophique* 6 (1950), 249-313.

Elorduy, Eleutherio, S.J. "El concepto objectivo en Suárez," *Pensamiento* 4, número extraordinario (1948), 335-423.

———. "Duns Scoti influxus in Francisci Suarez doctrinam," in *De doctrina Ioannis Duns Scoti*. Rome: Cura commissionis Scotisticae, 1968.

Eschweiler, Karl, "Die Philosophie der spanischen Spätscholastik auf der Universitäten des 17 Jahrhunderts," in *Spanische Forschungen der Görresgesellschaft*. Münster i.W., 1928. Pp. 251-325.

———. "Zur Geschichte der Barockscholastik," *Theologische Revue* 27-28 (1928-9), 337-344.

Fernández, C. *Metafísica del conocimiento en Suárez*. Madrid, 1954.

Fernández Burillo, Santiago. "Introducción a la teoría del conocimiento de Francisco Suárez," *Pensamiento* 48 (1992), 211-230.

Ferrater Mora, José. "Suarez and Modern Philosophy," *Journal of the History of Ideas* 14 (1953), 528-543.

Fichter, Joseph. *Man of Spain: Francis Suarez*. New York, 1940.

Gemmeke, E. *Die Metaphysik des sittlich Guten bei Franz Suarez.* Freiburg, 1965.

Giacon, Carlo, S.J. *Suarez.* Brescia, 1945.

Gilson, Etienne. *Being and Some Philosophers.* 2nd edition. Toronto, 1952.

Gnemmi, A. *Il fondamento metafisico. Analisi di struttura sulle Disputationes metaphysicae di F. Suarez.* Milan, 1969.

⎯⎯⎯⎯. "Fundamento metafisico e mediazione trascendentale nelle Disputationes metaphysicae di F. Suarez," *Rivista di filosofia neoscolastica* 58 (1966), 175-188.

Gómez Caffarena, José, S.J. "Sentido de la composición de ser y essencia en Suárez," *Pensamiento*, 15 (1959), 135-154.

Grabmann, Martin. "Die 'Disputationes Metaphysicae' des Franz Suarez in ihrer methodischen Eigenwart und Fortwirkung," in *Mittelalterisches Geistesleben*, Vol. I. München, 1926.

Gracia, Jorge J. E., "Francisco Suárez: The Man in History," *The American Catholic Philosophical Quarterly* 65 (1991), 259-266.

⎯⎯⎯⎯. "Suárez's Conception of Metaphysics: A Step in the Direction of Mentalism?" *The American Catholic Philosophical Quarterly* 65 (1991), 259-266.

Guthrie, Hunter, S.J. "The Metaphysics of Francis Suarez," *Thought* 16 (1941), 287-309.

Guy, Alain. "L'analogie de l'être selon Suarez," *Archives de philosophie* 42 (1979), 275-294.

Hellin, José, S.J. *La analogia del ser y el conocimiento de Dios en Suárez.* Madrid, 1947.

⎯⎯⎯⎯. "Abstracción del tercer grado y objeto de la metafísica," *Pensamiento* 4 (1948), 433-450.

⎯⎯⎯⎯. "Sobre el transito de la potentia activa al acto segun Suárez," *Razón y fe* 138 (1948), 353-407.

⎯⎯⎯⎯. "El ente real y los posibles en Suárez," *Espiritu* 10 (1961), 146-163.

⎯⎯⎯⎯. "Obtenación del concepto del ente, objeto de la metafísica," *Espiritu* 17 (1961), 135-154.

_____. "El concepto formal según Suárez," *Pensamiento* 18 (1962), 407-432.

Hoeres, W. "Francis Suarez and the Teaching of John Duns Scotus on Univocatio entis," in *John Duns Scotus (1265-1965)*. Ed. J. K. Ryan and B. M. Bonansea. Washington, 1965.

Iriarte, J. "La proyección sobre Europa de una gran metafísica, o Suárez en la filosofía de los dias del barocco," *Razón y fe* 138 (1948), 229-265.

Iturrioz, Jesús, S.J. *Estudios sobre la metafísica de Francisco Suárez.* Madrid, 1949.

Jansen, Bernhard, S.J., "Die Wesenart der Metaphysik des Suarez," *Scholastik* 15 (1940), 161-185.

_____. "Der Konservatismus in den Disputationes Metaphysicae des Suarez," *Gregorianum* 21 (1940), 452-481.

Junk, Nicholaus. *Die Bewegungslehre des Franz Suarez.* Innsbruck-Leipzig, 1938.

Lewalter, Ernst. *Spanische-jesuitische und deutschlutherische Metaphysik des 17 Jahrhunderts.* Hamburg, 1935.

Lohr, C. H., S.J. "Jesuit Aristotelianism and Sixteenth-Century Metaphysics," in *Paradosis: Studies in Memory of Edwin A. Quain, S.J..* New York, 1976. Pp. 203-220.

Marc, André, S.J. "L'idée de l'être chez St. Thomas et dans la scolastique postérieure," *Archives de philosophie* 10 (1933), 1-144.

Mesnard, P., S.J. "Comment Leibniz se trouva placé dans le sillage de Suarez," *Archives de philosophie* XVIII (1949), 7-32.

Millán-Puelles, Antonio. *Teoría del objeto puro.* Madrid: Rialp, 1990.

Neidl, Walter M. *Der Realitätsbegriff des Franz Suarez nach den Disputationes Metaphysicae.* München, 1966.

Noreña, Carlos G. "Ockham and Suárez on the Ontological Status of Universal Concepts," *The New Scholasticism* 55 (1981), 348-362.

_____. "Suárez on the Externality and Internality of Relations," *Cuadernos Salmantinos de Filosofía* 10 (1983), 183-195.

_____. "Heidegger on Suárez: The 1927 Marburg Lectures," *International Philosophical Quarterly* 23 (1983), 407-424.

_____. "Suárez and Spinoza: the Metaphysics of Moral Being," *Cuadernos Salmantinos de Filosofía* 12 (1985), 163-182.

_____. "Suárez and the Jesuits," *Cuadernos Salmantinos de Filosofía* 12 (1985), 267-286.

Owens, Joseph, C.Ss.R. "The Conclusion of the Prima Via," *The Modern Schoolman* 30 (1952-53), 33-53, 109-121, 203-215.

_____. "The Number of Terms in the Suarezian Discussion on Essence and Being," *The Modern Schoolman* 34 (1956-57), 147-191.

Rast, Max, S.J., "Die Possibilienlehre des Franz Suarez," *Scholastik* 10 (1935), 340-368.

Robinet, A. "Suarez dans l'oeuvre de Leibniz," *Cuadernos Salmantinos de Filosofía* 7 (1980), 269-284.

_____. "Suárez im Werk von Leibniz," *Studia Leibnitiana* 12 (1981), 76-96.

Roig Gironella, Juan, S.J. "La analogía del ser en Suárez," *Espiritu* (Barcelona) 36 (1987), 5-47.

Schneider, Marius, O.F.M. "Der angebliche philosophische Essentialismus des Suarez," *Wissenschaft und Weisheit* 24 (1961), 40-68.

Seigfried, Hans. *Wahrheit und Metaphysik bei Suarez* Bonn, 1967.

Sepich, Juan R. "Naturaleza de la filosofía primera o metafísica en Francisco Suárez," *Congreso Internacional de Filosofía Barcelona, 4-10 Octubre, 1948, Actas*. Madrid, 1949. III, 493-504.

Scorraille, Raoul de, S.J. *François Suarez de la Compagnie de Jesus*. 2 vols., Paris, 1911.

Solana, Marcial. *Historia de la filosofía española. Epoca del Renacimiento*, Tomo III. Madrid, 1941.

_____. "El principio y la causa según Suárez," *Revista del filosofía* 7 (1948), 409-431.

_____. "Doctrina de Suárez sobre el primer principio metafísico," *Pensamiento* 4, número extraordinario (1948), 245-275.

Tusquets Terrats, Juan. "François Suarez: sa métaphysique et sa criteriologie," in *Apports Hispaniques à la philosophie chrétienne de l'occident*. Louvain, 1962. Pp. 75-116.

Wells, Norman J. "Descartes and the Scholastics Briefly Revisited," *The New Scholasticism* 35 (1961), 172-190.

———. "Suarez, Historian and Critic of the Modal Distinction between Essential Being and Existential Being," *The New Scholasticism* 36 (1962), 419-444.

———. "Suarez on the Eternal Truths, I and II," *The Modern Schoolman* 58 (1980-81), 73-104, 159-174.

———. "Old Bottles and New Wine: A Rejoinder to J. C. Doig," *The New Scholasticism* 53 (1979-80), 515-523.

———. "Material Falsity in Descartes, Arnauld, and Suárez," *Journal of the History of Philosophy* 22 (1984), 25-50.

———. "Descartes' *Idea* and Its Sources," *American Catholic Philosophical Quarterly* 67 (1993), 513-535.

Werner, Karl. *Franz Suarez und die Scholastik der letzten Jahrhunderts*. 2 vols. Regensburg, 1889.

Wundt, Max. *Die deutsche Schulmetaphysik des 17 Jahrhunderts*. Tubingen, 1939.

Yela Utrilla, Juan. "El tema de la verdad en la metafísica de Suárez," *Revista de filosofía* 7 (1948), 659-692.

———. "El ente de razón en Suárez," *Pensamiento* 4, número extraordinario (1948), 271-303.

Zubimendi Martínez, Julián. "La teoría de las distinciones de Suárez y Descartes," *Pensamiento* 40 (1984), 179-202.

# Index of Names

Aegidius Romanus: 11, 101
Alarcon, Diego: 29
Albert the Great, St.: 11
Alcorta, J.: 91
Alejandro, J.: 11
Alexander of Aphrodisias: 11, 58
Alexander of Hales: 11
Alluntis, F.: 2, 63
Alvarez, Baltasar: 4, 6
Ambrose, St.: 95
Andrés Marcos, T.: 7, 13
Anselm, St.: 11
Antonio Andreas: 3, 14, 29, 59
Aquinas, St. Thomas: 4-6, 8, 11, 19, 29-30, 34, 41, 58, 61-63, 66, 75, 80, 84-87, 89, 91, 93, 95, 112, 114
Aristotle: 7-9, 11, 18-20, 22, 25, 29, 34-36, 40-41, 43-44, 49, 58, 60-63, 65, 79, 84, 86-87, 95-96, 99, 101-103, 105-106, 108-110, 112, 119
Arriaga, R. de: 29
Ashworth, E. J.: 44, 109
Astrain, A.: 3
Augustine, St.: 11, 30, 78, 87
Aureoli, Petrus: 11
Averroes: 11, 41, 62-63
Avicenna: 11

Bañez, Domingo: 2
Bellarmine, St. Robert: 3
Bergson, H.: 22, 46, 53
Berkeley, G.: 52
Berton, C.: 6, 56, 108
Biel, Gabriel: 11
Boethius: 11

Bonaventure, St.: 11, 43
Boyer, C.: 25
Brentano, F.: 20, 53
Buridan, John: 43
Burns, J. P.: 37

Cabero: 34
Cajetan (Thomas del Vio): 11, 22, 34, 60, 62-63, 86, 94, 109
Cano, Melchior: 2
Capreolus, John: 11, 22, 60, 86, 101
Cardillo Villalpendo, Gaspar: 44
Chisholm, R.: 20, 28
Coinimbricenses: 22
Compton Carleton, T.: 24, 29
Conze, E.: 124
Copleston, F.: 14
Cornford, F. M.: 18
Courtney, W. J.: 112
Courtine, J.-F.: 14
Cronin, T.: 124
Cruz, M.: 124

Damascene, St. John: 11
Davis, D.: 9
De Rhodes, George: 22, 28
De Rijk, L.: 18
Deely, J.: 22, 54
Descartes, René: 4, 8, 13-4, 52
Descoqs, P.: 11
Desharnais, R. P.: 111
Deuringer, K.: 6
Deza, D.: 22
Dibon, P.: 13
Doig, J.: 124
Doyle, J.: 9, 23, 27, 48, 57, 62, 66,

124
Drouin, P.: 124
Duhr, B.: 12, 124
Duns Scotus: 11, 26, 63, 71, 73, 81, 112
Durandus de Saint Pourçain: 11, 26-27, 63, 81

Elias de Tejada, F.: 7
Elorduy, E.: 125
Eschweiler, K.: 13

Fernández, C.: 125
Fernández, Burillo: 125
Ferrara, Sylvester de: 11, 22, 60, 86, 101
Ferrater Mora, J.: 8
Fichter, J: 1-5, 7
Flanders, Dominic of: 12
Fonseca, Pedro de: 11, 44, 108, 115
Francis of Mayronnes: 21, 59, 64
Frege, G.: 43, 53

Gemmeke, E.: 126
Giacon, C.: 18, 111
Gilen, L.: 13
Gilson, E.: 4, 8, 12-15, 27, 59
Goclenius, R.: 50
Gómez Caffarena, J.: 10, 126
Grabmann, M.: 8, 14
Gracia, J.: 1, 9
Gregory Nazianzen: 11
Grosseteste, R.: 8
Grossmann, R.: 20
Grotius, Hugo: 13
Guthrie, H.: 11
Guy, A.: 126

Heidegger, M.: 13, 31, 53
Hellin, J.: 49
Henry of Ghent: 11
Hervaeus Natalis: 11
Hurtado de Mendoza, Pedro: 23, 27-29, 34, 38
Husserl, E.: 53

Iriarte, J.: 7, 13-14
Iturrioz, J.: 4, 11

James I, King: 7, 9-10
Jansen, B.: 127
Javellus, Chrysostomus: 11, 101
Junk, N.: 14

Kant, I.: 15, 20, 24, 34, 53

La Palu, Peter of: 12
Larequi, J.: 13
Leibniz, Gottfried: 14, 52
Lewalter, E.: 13
Linsky, L.: 43, 53
Lohr, C.: 127
Longpré, E.: 8
Luther, Martin: 13, 111-112
Lychetus, Franciscus: 12
Lynch, J.: 3
Lynch, R.: 29

Madrigal, Pedro: 4
Mahieu, L.: 11, 14
Major, John: 43
Malou, M.: 3
Mancio, Juan: 2
Mangold, M.: 23
Maréchal, J.: 11
Marsilius of Inghen: 11
Maurer, A.: 8, 14, 27, 70
McKenna, C.: 2
McKeon, C. K.: 8
Medina, Bartolomeo de: 2
Meinong, A.: 20-21, 28, 52
Melanchthon, Philip: 13
Mesnard, P.: 14, 127
Millán-Puelles, A.: 14, 127
Mirandulanus, B.: 59
Molina, Luis de: 3

Monnot, P.: 1, 4-6
Mora, J. F.: 8, 13
Muñoz Delgado, V.: 109

Nifo, Agostino: 9, 99, 101
Noreña, C.: 1, 13

Ockham, William of: 11, 43, 53, 112
Ovid: 22
Ovideo, F. de: 29
Owens, J.: 10

Parmenides: 17
Paul V, Pope: 4
Pegs, A.: 19
Pereña, L.: 6-7
Pernoud, M. A.: 112
Plato: 11, 17-19, 33, 53
Poinsot, John (John of St. Thomas): 22, 34, 52
Powell, R.: 22
Pseudo Dionysius: 11
Pusey, E.: 78

Quine, W. V.: 43, 53

Ramus, Pierre: 8
Renaut, Juan y Andrés: 7
Rhodes, G. de: 49
Richard of Middleton: 11, 29, 111
Riedl, J.: 2
Rivière, E. M.: 8
Risse, W.: 58
Roig Gironella, J.: 31, 128
Ross, J. F.: 9
Ross, W. D.: 19
Rubio, Antonio; 28-29, 34, 44, 51
Ruiz Moreno, I.: 13
Russell, B.: 20, 43, 53

Santos-Escudero, C.: 123
Sartre, J. P.: 31
Sassen, F.: 13
Scheibler, C.: 49-50
Schneider, M.: 128
Schopenhauer, A.: 14
Scorraille, R. De: 1-7, 13, 29
Seigfried, H.: 128
Sepich, J.: 128
Serna, P.: 34
Simplicius: 11
Socrates: 17, 43
Solana, M.: 4
Sommervogel, C.: 4
Soncinas, Paulus: 11, 22, 60, 62, 67, 86, 99, 101
Soto, Domingo de: 2, 11, 22, 44, 79
Sotomayor, Pedro de: 2
Suárez, Juan: 1

Thomas of York: 8
Timpler, C.: 50
Toletus, Franciscus: 79

Valencia, Gregory of: 2
Vázquez, Gabriel: 27, 29, 72
Vitoria, Francisco de: 2
Vollert, C.: 9

Wells, N.: 10-12
Weisheipl, J.: 62
Werner, K.: 129
Wietrowski, M.: 24
Wolff, Christian: 14-15
Wolfson, H.: 12
Wundt, M.: 13

Yela-Utrilla, J.: 23

Zubimendi Martinez, J.: 129

# Index of Terms

Absence: 31-32, 45-47, 55, 100, 113
Action, Immanent and Transient: 37, 96
Acts of Intellect: 26, 28, 51, 72-73, 99, 119
   Conception: 26, 46, 51, 60, 64, 81-82, 87, 94, 112, 116, 122
   Judgment: 18, 23, 26, 39, 47, 51, 82-84, 106, 116
   Reasoning: 26, 44, 51, 55, 64, 71, 73, 80, 94-96, 100, 106, 112-113
Ampliation: 108-109
Analogy: 18, 23, 35, 57, 60, 62, 65-66, 89-90, 113, 117-118
Angels: 5, 26, 46-47, 69, 79, 84, 100, 115-116
Antecedent: 26, 51, 56, 70, 72, 85, 90, 99, 121
Aptitude: 40-42, 45, 100, 102-103, 105-107

Being an Orphan: 32, 89
Being as True: 18
Being in the Truth of a Proposition: 40, 61, 101
Bergsonian "Pseudo-Problems": 53
Blindness: 22, 29, 31, 39, 41-42, 44-45, 60, 63, 75, 86-87, 100-101, 103-106, 108, 110
Buyer and Seller: 50, 120

Categories and Beings of Reason: 32-35, 37-38, 43, 90-95, 97, 111-113

Causes of Beings of Reason: 21, 25-26, 28, 58, 75
Chimera: 22-24, 27-28, 33-34, 38, 42-44, 46, 48-50, 63-64, 79, 90-92, 97, 107-109, 118
Common Concept of Being: 22, 60, 65
Common Name of Being: 22-23, 60, 65
Consequent: 46, 51, 70, 121
Contradictories: 19, 38-39, 42-43, 79, 99, 106
Contraries: 105
Controversies: 3
Copula: 39-40, 43-44, 51, 101, 107-108, 121
Creation *ex nihilo*: 46, 110

Darkness: 29, 75-76, 86-87, 100-101, 103, 111
Deafness: 46, 110, 115
Death: 31, 89, 112
Definition: 51, 63, 120-121
Diminished Being: 27, 70
Division of Beings of Reason: 29, 32-34, 38, 40, 46-48, 58, 61, 65, 84-86, 89-93, 97, 102, 117-118
Dominion: 37, 91, 95

Education of Suárez: 1-3
Error and Falsehood: 53
Evil: 6, 9, 22, 31, 47, 53, 86, 104, 115, 123
Excluded Middle: 42-43, 105-107
Existence of Beings of Reason: 21-22, 26, 60-61, 63-64

Existentialism: 31, 53
Extrinsic Denomination: 9, 17, 26-28, 33, 36-37, 50-51, 63, 69, 71-75, 77-78, 95-97, 119-121

Faculty for Neighing: 41-42, 46, 100, 114
Fame: 33, 36-37, 95
Fecundity of the Intellect: 25, 64
Fictions: 34, 40, 42, 53, 59, 83, 92, 107, 122
Flying Ox: 97
Formal Concept: 26, 62, 68, 74
Foundation of Beings of Reason: 31, 33-35, 41, 47-51, 60, 66, 73, 75, 77, 79, 87-88, 91-93, 99, 104-105, 117-121

*Gegenstand Überhaupt*: 24
*Gegenstandstheorie*: 20
Genus: 9, 21, 33, 51, 69, 88-89, 92, 103-104, 120-122
Goat-stag: 18-20, 23-24, 29, 38, 48, 109, 118
God and Beings of Reason: 26, 28-29, 70-71, 80-84
Golden Mountain: 28, 79

Homeless Objects: 20, 52
Honor: 36-37, 95
Husband and Wife: 50, 120

Ideas: 52, 80
Identity: 31, 49, 51, 72, 88, 119, 121
Imaginary Space: 33, 35-36, 46, 49, 90, 95, 109, 114
Imaginary Time: 36, 46, 48, 108
Imagination: 19, 26, 28, 73, 79, 83
Impossibles: 63-64
Influence of Suárez: 5, 12-15, 52-53
Intelligibility: 19-20, 22, 24, 35, 42, 57, 63

Intentional Being: 23
Intentionality Theory: 15, 53

Jurisdiction: 3, 33, 37, 91, 95

Life of Suárez: 1-3
Literary Fictions: 53
Logical Intentions: 51, 120
Logical Fictions: 53

Master and Slave: 50, 120
Mean: 51
Measurement: 36, 49-50, 91, 119
Meinongian Entities: 20
Metaphor: 23-24, 30, 87, 116

Nature of Beings of Reason: 21, 58, 63, 67, 80, 89-90
Necessity and Contingency: 42, 45, 47, 80, 107-108, 110, 116
Negation and Privation as Beings of Reason: 45-47, 111-116
Negation and Privation in Things: 40-45, 98-111
Negation, Negative and Infinite: 44, 107
Negations, Simple and Complex: 45, 47, 75, 97, 106, 113, 116
Nothing: 4, 17-19, 22-24, 31, 35-37, 41-43, 46, 53, 64, 66, 68-71, 74-75, 77, 80, 96, 106, 108, 110, 113-114

Object in General: 24
Objective Being: 23, 68-69, 84
Objective Concept: 51, 68, 74, 83, 120, 122

Phenomenology: 53
Popperian Third World: 53
Predicate: 38-39, 42-44, 51, 60, 64, 77, 100-101, 105-108, 120-121
Predication: 39, 43, 84, 87, 100

Priority and Posteriority: 27, 48, 118
Privations: 10, 18, 21, 25, 29-33, 38-42, 45-48, 58, 61, 64-65, 70, 76, 80-82, 84-86, 88-90, 92, 95, 97-116
Privation in a Subject: 29-33
Privation as Principle of Change: 45, 86, 103, 109-110
Prohibited Beings: 38, 42, 64

Quasi-Being: 20-21
Quasi-cause: 21, 25-26, 67
Quasi-difference: 93
Quasi-disposition: 113
Quasi-Essence: 21, 105
Quasi-matter: 67
Quasi-passion: 76, 113
Quasi-place: 46
Quasi-substance: 46
Quasi-time: 46
Quasi-transcendence: 25

Real Being: 10, 17, 20-28, 30, 35-37, 47-50, 53, 57-63, 65-66, 68, 70, 72-76, 85-87, 90, 92, 94, 107, 109, 117-118, 121
Relations
    Real and Rational: 10, 21-22, 25, 28-32, 37, 47-50, 60, 63-65, 70, 72-73, 75-76, 78, 80-81, 84-85, 87-89, 96-97, 112, 116-122
    Conditions: 47-49, 99, 117-118, 122
    Adventitious: 47, 94
    Categorical and Transcendental: 47, 72, 94
    *Secundum esse* and *secundum dici*: 31, 88
Reputation: 33, 90, 95

Scientific Constructs: 50
Second Intentions: 21, 51-52, 76-77, 121-122
Secondary Intelligibility: 35, 57
Self-contradiction: 46
Semiotics: 19, 22, 52-53
Senses: 28, 77-78
Signification: 19, 44, 49-50, 53, 60, 105, 108-109
Silence: 31
Similarity: 51, 73, 111, 118-119
*Sinn und Bedeutung*: 43, 53
Species: 9, 21, 25, 33, 36-37, 41, 51, 59, 67, 84, 89-91, 100, 102-103, 110, 115, 120-122
Square Circle: 23
Suárez as Historian: 12
Subject: 26, 51, 77, 120-121
Subject and limits of Metaphysics: 9-10, 17, 19-22, 27, 57-58
Supertranscendence: 53, 125
Supposition: 44, 53

Theory of Descriptions: 53
Time: Extrinsic and Intrinsic: 36, 91
Transcendentals: 13, 21, 24, 47, 58, 72, 94
Truth and Meaning as Functions of Being: 17, 24

Universal: 9, 26, 33, 45, 51, 69-70, 76-78, 92, 120-123, 127

Void: 21, 35-36, 58

Will: 28, 69, 70, 73, 78-79
Works of Suárez: 3-12

# Mediæval Philosophical Texts in Translation
# Complete List

## Under the Editorship of Gerard Smith, S.J.

Grosseteste: *On Light.* Clare Riedl, Tr. ISBN 0-87462-201-8 (Translation No. 1, 1942). 28 pp. $5.

St. Augustine: *Against the Academicians.* Mary Patricia Garvey, R.S.M., Tr. ISBN 0-87462-202-6. (Translation No. 2, 1942). 94 pp. $10

Pico Della Mirandola: *Of Being and Unity.* Victor M. Hamm, Tr. ISBN 0-87462-203-4. (Translation No. 3, 1943). 40 pp. $10

Francis Suarez: *On the Various Kinds of Distinctions.* Cyril Vollert, S.J., Tr. ISBN 0-87462-204-2. (Translation No. 4, 1947). 72 pp. $10

St. Thomas Aquinas: *On Spiritual Creatures.* Mary C. Fitzpatrick, Tr. ISBN 0-87462-205-0. (Translation No. 5, 1949). 144 pp. $15

Guigo: *Meditations of Guigo.* John J. Jolin, S.J., Tr. ISBN 0-87462-206-9. (Translation No. 6, 1951). 96 pp. $10

Giles of Rome: *Theorems on Existence and Essence.* Michael V. Murray, S.J., Tr. ISBN 0-87462-207-7. (Translation No. 7, 1953). 128 pp. $15

John of St. Thomas: *Outlines of Formal Logic.* Francis C. Wade, S.J., Tr. ISBN 0-87462-208-5. (Translation No. 8, 1955). 144 pp. $15

Hugh of St. Victor: *Soliloquy in the Earnest Money of the Soul.* Kevin Herbert, Tr. ISBN 0-87462-209-3. (Translation No. 9, 1956). 48 pp. $5

## Under the Editorship of James H. Robb

St. Thomas Aquinas: *On Charity.* Lottie Kendzierski, Tr. ISBN 0-87462-210-7. (Translation No. 10, 1960). 120 pp. $15

Aristotle: *On Interpretation: Commentary by St. Thomas and Cajetan.* Jean T. Oesterle, Tr. ISBN 0-87462-211-5. (Translation No. 11, 1962). 288 pp. $20

Desiderius Erasmus of Rotterdam: *On Copia of Words and Ideas.* Donald B. King and H. David Rix, Tr. ISBN 0-87462-212-3. (Translation No. 12, 1963). 124 pp. $15

Peter of Spain: *Tractatus Syncategorematum and Selected Anonymous Treatises.* Joseph P. Mullally and Roland Houde, Tr. ISBN 0-87462-213-1. (Translation No. 13, 1964). 168 pp. $15

Cajetan: *Commentary on St. Thomas Aquinas' On Being and Essence.* Lottie Kendzierski and Francis C. Wade, S.J., Tr. ISBN 0-87462-214-X. (Translation No. 14, 1965). 366 pp. $20

Suárez: *Disputation VI, On Formal and Universal Unity.* James F. Ross, Tr. ISBN 0-87462-215-8. (Translation. No. 15, 1965). 132 pp. $15

St. Thomas, Siger de Brabant, St. Bonaventure: *On the Eternity of the World.* Cyril Vollert, S.J., Lottie Kendzierski, and Paul Byrne, Tr. ISBN 0-87462-216-6. (Translation No. 16, 1965). 132 pp. $15

Geoffrey of Vinsauf: *Instruction in the Method and Art of Speaking and Versifying.* Roger P. Parr, Tr. ISBN 0-87462-217-4. (Translation No. 17, 1968). 128 pp. $15

Liber De Pomo: *The Apple, or Aristotle's Death.* Mary F. Rousseau, Tr. ISBN 0-87462-218-2. (Translation No. 18, 1968). 96 pp. $5

St. Thomas Aquinas: *On the Unity of the Intellect against the Averroists.* Beatrice H. Zedler, Tr. ISBN 0-87462-219-0. (Translation No. 19, 1969). 96 pp. $10

Nicholas of Autrecourt. *The Universal Treatise.* Leonard L. Kennedy, C.S.B., Tr. ISBN 0-87462-220-4. (Translation No. 20, 1971). 174 pp. $15
Pseudo-Dionysius Areopagite: *The Divine Names and Mystical Theology.* John D. Jones, Tr. ISBN 0-87462-221-2. (Translation No. 21, 1980). 320 pp. $25
Matthew of Vendome: *Ars Versificatoria.* Roger P. Parr, Tr. ISBN 0-87462-222-0. (Translation No. 22, 1981). 150 pp. $15
Francis Suárez. *On Individuation.* Jorge J.E. Gracia, Tr. ISBN 0-87462-223-9. (Translation No. 23, 1982). 304 pp. $35
Francis Suárez: *On the Essence of Finite Being as Such, on the Existence of That Essence and Their Distinction.* Norman J. Wells, Tr. ISBN 0-87462-224-7. (Translation No. 24, 1983). 248 pp. $20
*The Book of Causes (Liber De Causis).* Dennis J. Brand, Tr. ISBN 0-87462-225-5. (Translation No. 25, 1984). 56 pp. $5
Giles of Rome: *Errores Philosophorum.* John O. Riedl, Tr. Intro. by Josef Koch. ISBN 0-87462-429-0. (Translation No. 26, 1944). 136 pp. $10
St. Thomas Aquinas: *Questions on the Soul.* James H. Robb, Tr. ISBN 0-87462-226-3. (Translation No. 27, 1984). 285 pp. $25

## Under the Editorship of Richard C. Taylor

William of Auvergne. *The Trinity.* Roland J. Teske, S.J. and Francis C. Wade, S.J. ISBN 0-87462-231-X 286 pp. (Translation No. 28, 1989) 1989 $20

## Under the Editorship of Roland J. Teske, S.J.

Hugh of St. Victor. *Practical Geometry.* Frederick A. Homann, S.J., Tr. ISBN 0-87462-232-8 92 pp. (Translation No. 29, 1991) $10
William of Auvergne. *The Immortality of the Soul.* Roland J. Teske, S.J., Tr. ISBN 0-87462-233-6 72 pp. (Translation No. 30, 1992) $10
Dietrich of Freiberg.*Treatise of the Intellect and the Intelligible.* M. L. Führer, Tr. ISBN 0-87462-234-4 135 pp. (Translation No. 31, 1992) $15
Henry of Ghent. *Quodlibetal Questions on Free Will.* Roland J. Teske, S.J., Tr. ISBN 0-87462-234-4 135 pp. (Translation No. 32, 1993) $15
Francisco Suárez, S.J. *On Beings of Reason. Metaphysical Disputation LIV.* John P. Doyle, Tr. ISBN 0-87462-236-0 170 pp. (Translation No. 33, 1995) $20
Francisco De Vitoria, O.P. *On Homicide,* and *Commentary on Thomas Aquinas: Summa theologiae IIaIIae, 64.* Edited and Translated by John Doyle. ISBN 0-87462-237-9. 280 pp. (Translation No. 34, 1997) $30.
William of Auvergne. *The Universe of Creatures.* Edited, Translated, and with an Introduction by Roland J. Teske, S.J. ISBN 0-87462-238-7. 235 pp. (Translation No. 35, 1998) $25.
Francis Suarez, S.J. *On the Formal Cause of Substance. Metaphysical Disputation XV.* Translated by John Kronen & Jeremiah Reedy. Introduction & Explanatory Notes by John Kronen. ISBN 0-87462-239-5. 218 pp. (Translation No. 36, 2000) $25.
William of Auvergne. *The Soul.* Translated from the Latin with an Introduction and Notes by Roland J. Teske, S.J. ISBN 0-87462-240-9. 516 pp. (Translation No. 37, 2000) $50.
*The Conimbricenses: Some Questions on Signs.* Translated with Introduction and Notes by John P. Doyle.ISBN 0-87462-241-7. 217 pp. (Translation No. 38, 2001) $25.

Dominicus Gundissalinus. *The Procession of the World (De processione mundi)*. Translated from the Latin with an Introduction & Notes by John A. Laumakis. ISBN 0-87462-242-5. 87 pp. $10 (Translation No. 39, 2002).

Francisco Suárez. *A Commentary on Aristotle's Metaphysics or "A Most Ample Index to the Metaphysics of Aristotle" (Index locupletissimus in Metaphysicam Aristotelis)*. Translated with an Introduction & Notes by John P. Doyle. (Translation No. 40, 2003)

Mediæval Philosophical Texts in Translation

Roland J. Teske, S.J., Editor

This series originated at Marquette University in 1942, and with revived interest in Mediæval studies is read internationally with steadily increasing popularity. Available in attractive, durable, colored soft covers. Volumes priced from $5 to $50 each. Complete Set [0-87462-200-X] receives a 40% discount. John Riedl's *A Catalogue of Renaissance Philosophers*, hardbound with red cloth, is an ideal reference companion title (sent free with purchase of complete set). New standing orders receive a 30% discount and a free copy of the Riedl volume. Regular reprinting keeps all volumes available. Recent volumes are also available as ebooks.

See our web page: http://www.marquette.edu/mupress/
Order from:
  Marquette University Press
  30 Amberwood Parkway
  Ashland OH 44805
     Tel. 800-247-6553 Fax: 419-281-6883

Editorial Address for **Mediæval Philosophical Texts in Translation**:
Roland J. Teske, S.J., Editor MPTT
Department of Philosophy
Marquette Univesity
Box 1881
Milwaukee WI 53201-1881

Marquette University Press office:
Marquette University Press
Dr. Andrew Tallon, Director
Box 1881
Milwaukee WI 53201-1881
     Tel: (414) 288-7298 FAX: (414) 288-3300
         Internet: andrew.tallon@marquette.edu
     Web Page: **http://www.marquette.edu/mupress/**